CREATING FASHION

Betty Foster

THAMES MACDONALD

© Macdonald & Co (Publishers) Ltd
and Thames Television 1983
Text and patterns © Betty Foster 1983

First published in Great Britain in 1983
by Macdonald & Co (Publishers) Ltd
London & Sydney

A member of BPCC plc

ISBN 0 356 07892 2 (hardback)
ISBN 0 356 09707 2 (paperback)

Printed and bound in Great Britain
by Hazell Watson & Viney Limited,
Member of the BPCC Group,
Aylesbury, Bucks

Macdonald & Co (Publishers) Ltd
Maxwell House
74 Worship Street
London EC2A 2EN

Editor
Bridget Daly

Design
Carole Ash
Kathy Gummer

Illustrations
Jil Shipley
Linda Taylor

Picture Research
Suzanne Williams

Production
Sue Mead

CONTENTS

INTRODUCTION

From the time when humans first covered their naked bodies, 'fashion' has been evolving. The type of clothing being worn at any one time in history has been dependent on the demands of climate and the type of material available. The designs arrived at reflected the status of, or the work undertaken by, the wearer. Animal skins, leaves and tree bark were the first coverings used. The development of spinning and weaving in many primitive civilizations brought about the first pieces of cloth that could be wrapped or draped around the body. Rough home-spun material using the wool from sheep, goats and other animals gave warmth for colder climates. Flax, cotton and silks produced light, and often more elaborate clothing. Each civilization produced its own ethnic fabrics, painting, embroidering them and using vegetable dyes to change the colour of the raw cloth.

Over the centuries invaders, crusaders and merchant travellers moved over land and sea, carrying knowledge and skills from one civilization to another. Sewing methods and equipment needed to make garments became a part of the world's industrial history. Before the sixteenth century, fashion tended to take sixty years or more to change and as this process speeded up to the present day, the average man and woman has invariably worn a combination of several fashion changes.

The first cutting of fabric was into the T-shaped tunic _ the forerunner of the present day T-shirt _ which was the first attempt to cut cloth to fit the body and this simple shape has been constantly adapted to fit the needs of the wearer.

Fashion designing began when individual styles were developed to create a new image. Changing the way the garment looked by seaming variations _ the jig-sawing of the basic shape _ altering the proportions to draw attention to those areas of the body chosen for emphasis, and gradually arriving at a closer fit, all contributed to the evolution of fashion.

From the Industrial Revolution in the latter half of the eighteenth century, gentlemen in particular were adopting more varied styles of dress, suiting time of day, town or country wear, formal or informal and women's fashions have continued to evolve on this basis since that time.

With the closer fitting of garments, the measurements of the wearer began to be of prime importance. Using the wearer as a model achieved the correct fitting and once done, the tailor or dressmaker would make a master pattern of the client from which they could make other garments without the necessity for long and tedious fitting sessions. For those who could not afford to pay for these services, fashion changes were less involved, because the 'home dressmaker' would unpick a worn-out dress and copy it in a new fabric, learning instinctively how to alter size, how to cut slightly differently and how to make the best use of every scrap of fabric available.

It was not until 1917 that the paper pattern industry, as we know it today, really gained impetus on the mass market. From a survey taken then, an average size chart was produced and the printed paper pattern became the main method of creating instant fashion, which could be made at home. However, because no two figures are alike, the standard size chart presented an immediate problem of how to deal with the non-standard figure. Ideally, when the potential market for home sewing was becoming obvious, the education authorities should have anticipated the need to teach any prospective dressmaker not only garment construction skills, but how each person could get an accurate master pattern of themselves and then how to adapt this accurate map of themselves into current fashion _ exactly as the dressmaker worked before printed patterns.

The master pattern in this book can be obtained by following the instructions on pages 30–43 or you can write off for Betty Foster's printed Teaching Master Pattern and simply correct it to your figure.

Two things become obvious as the book progresses; firstly that dress design is hardly ever original and secondly that with a good master pattern that fits, you can create any garment that you want from the fashion of today.

It is recommended that you study the essential reading pages at the end of the book before proceeding.

DRAPING IN
GREECE AND ROME

'Fashion' has not always been beautiful, because the idea of beauty changes. It has often been a 'status symbol' where the wealthy displayed their affluence in the clothes and jewellery that they wore and, in more modern times, the attitude of people to society is often reflected in the clothes they wear. In the classical world of Greece and Rome the draping of lengths of fabric formed the basis of the garments being worn, as indeed is still done by the Indian sari and other national costumes. Much of our information on the costume of these periods is derived from statues and paintings. The use of woven fabrics in wool, linen and silk predominated, and the cloth was used in its woven width and length, either by draping, or by folding the cloth around the body and throwing it over the shoulder to form a sleeve, often leaving one arm bare. There was little difference in the costume for men and women, except that the length shortened for the male population to give greater freedom of movement. The Roman *toga* was usually a length of cloth up to three times the height of the wearer, and it was often worn over the Greek *chiton*, which formed the undergarment.

The author and publishers would like to stress that the history of dress is a highly complex subject. The descriptions given in the following 32 pages provide a general idea of historical dress and are presented in a way that would help the modern dressmaker to imitate them.
They are not to be taken as a learned account of the history of costume.

GREEK CHITON

The Greek *chiton* was a beautifully simple garment, worn by both men and women at different lengths. Two pieces of uncut fabric were simply sewn at the sides and held with clasps to form the neck and armhole openings. The waist was gathered in with a girdle.

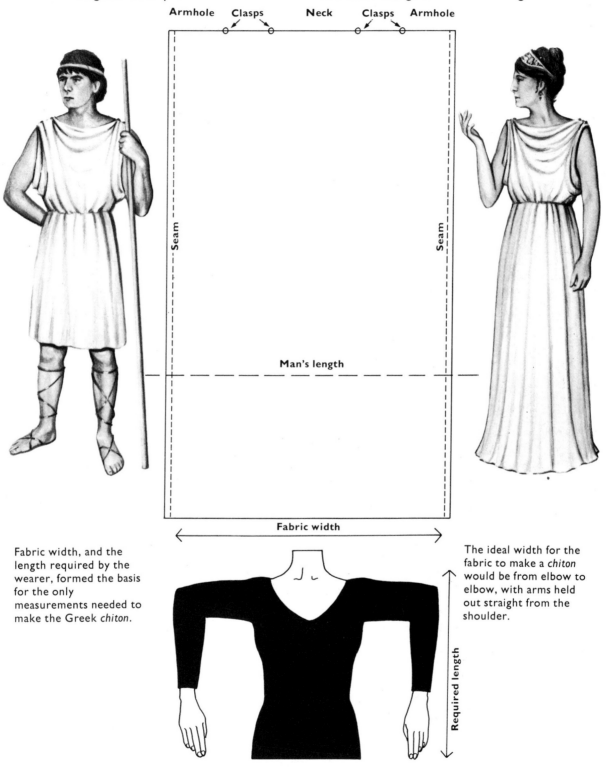

Armhole   Clasps   Neck   Clasps   Armhole

Seam

Seam

Man's length

Fabric width

Fabric width, and the length required by the wearer, formed the basis for the only measurements needed to make the Greek *chiton*.

The ideal width for the fabric to make a *chiton* would be from elbow to elbow, with arms held out straight from the shoulder.

Required length

SIMPLE ROMAN TUNIC

The Roman dress was very similar to the Greek, although slightly more simple and using less fabric in the width. The women's dress was called a *stola*, and because it was slimmer than the Greek *chiton* other fabrics were often draped over it either for warmth or elaboration. Roman men wore either a *chiton* or a simple full-length garment seamed on the shoulder to form a primitive tunic – the fore-runner of the magyar sleeve. With the full length tunic he wore the *toga*, which is a semicircle of fabric about 4.5 metres in diameter draped and arranged about the body.

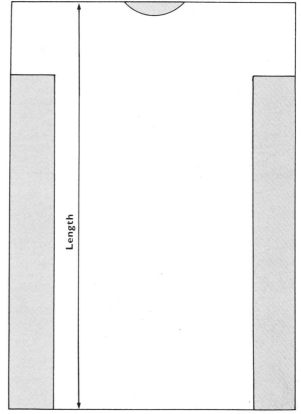

Two lengths of fabric cut to form sleeves and also to reduce the amount of fabric around the body.

It is doubtful if measurements were in fact used, the width of fabric available would be accepted and gathered in with a girdle, to be taken in to the body size.

The diagram of the simple toga is from the Early Roman period, as opposed to the more complicated Late Imperial toga in the photograph. The simple toga was draped over the left shoulder so that the end reached the floor in front and the other end passed around the body and was flung over the left shoulder again to drape down the back.

THE TUNIC

By the early Middle Ages the tunic had become the main garment worn by males and females young and old, and it can be found in the costume history of every civilization. The type of fabric used, and the richness of the decoration and accessories denoted the status of the wearer. The cutting out was simple, the stitching nominal, and the measurements easily calculated. Yet it was from this point that the dress-making and fashion industry started to develop.

Sleeve length   ½ Body width & movement ease   Sleeve length

½ Body width plus movement ease

ONE-PIECE TUNIC

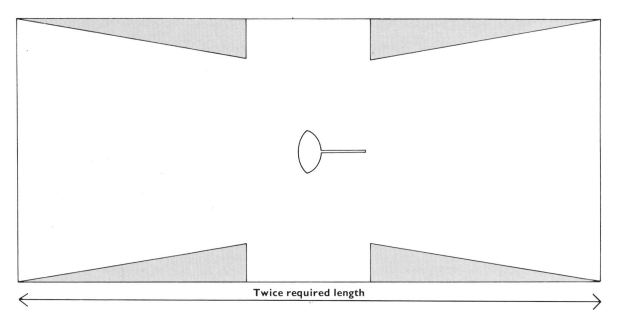

Twice required length

Made from one length of material, with a hole cut for the neck, this tunic could also be cut to fit closer to the body at the top, whilst leaving the fullness at the hem to allow for movement.

Because the neck was cut to fit close, this made an opening necessary to get the head through. This opening would be held together with a clasp or by lacing.

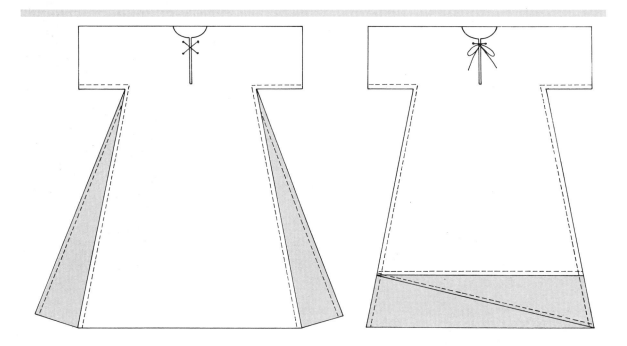

Fabric was never wasted, and 'left-over' sections cut from the sides could lengthen the garment or be added to the sides to give additional hem fullness.

THE JIG SAW TUNIC

Once the possibility of using small pieces of joined fabric to form the tunic shape had evolved, a whole new concept emerged. Expensive fabrics and different textures could be mixed. The development of dyeing processes applied to the natural wools, linens and cottons gave added interest. The various skills of embroidery, trimming and painting could be applied to sections of a garment before they were joined. Sectioning the work meant that more than one person could be involved in making a garment. This was the beginning of the clothing industry which led to the huge factories of today, where the finished garment only emerges as the pieces from different machines are brought together.

JAPANESE KIMONO

This garment is again based on the minimum measurements of length and width required and no shaped cutting is involved. The obvious rectangular shapes allowed for considerable versatility of fabric use.

The traditional Japanese sleeve was formed by stitching the bottom of the sleeve, as illustrated, leaving an opening for the arm. Both the underarm of the sleeve and the corresponding body seam of the kimono, are left open to allow freedom of movement.

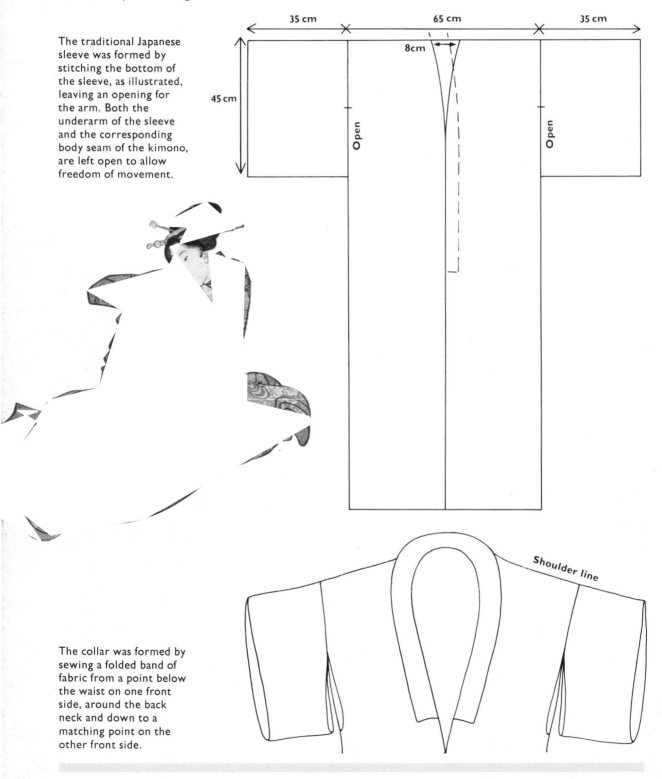

The collar was formed by sewing a folded band of fabric from a point below the waist on one front side, around the back neck and down to a matching point on the other front side.

SHAPING TO THE BODY

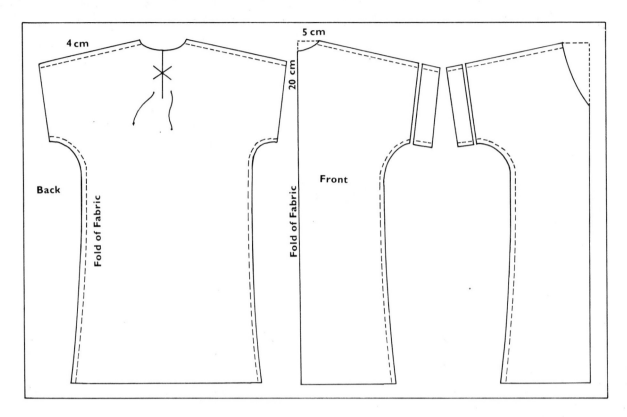

4 cm

Back

Fold of Fabric

5 cm

20 cm

Fold of Fabric

Front

The sloping of the shoulder and the closer body fitting produced more curves than the previous use of rectangles only, so that less fabric was being gathered in at the waist. More decorative belts and ornaments could be worn because they would not now be hidden by fabric.

The first separate sleeves began to appear possibly because the fabric width did not allow for it to be cut all-in-one with the body. The front and back of the first tunics were practically identical but changes in necklines brought about separate front and back cutting.

PATTERN ADAPTING BEGINS

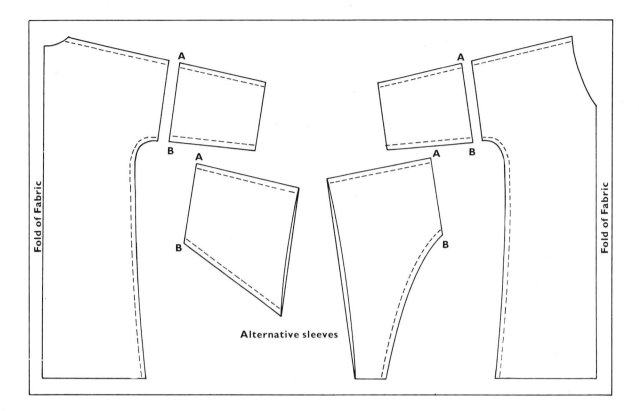

Fold of Fabric

Fold of Fabric

Alternative sleeves

Once the separate cutting of the sleeve was introduced, the first pattern adapting began. The endless possibilities of change simply by varying the sleeve, can still be seen in the fashion collections of today.

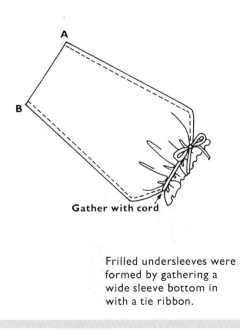

Gather with cord

Frilled undersleeves were formed by gathering a wide sleeve bottom in with a tie ribbon.

SIMPLE FRONT OPENING

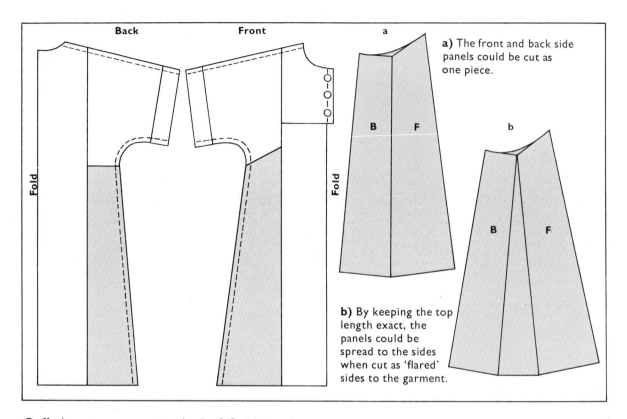

Back   Front   a

Fold

a) The front and back side panels could be cut as one piece.

B F

b

B F

b) By keeping the top length exact, the panels could be spread to the sides when cut as 'flared' sides to the garment.

Cuffs became a new method of finishing the sleeves and a more sophisticated method of front-opening created another use for the jig-saw cutting of the tunic.

Two overlapped pieces allowed buttons and buttonholes to be used.

THE MAGYAR TUNIC AND COLLAR

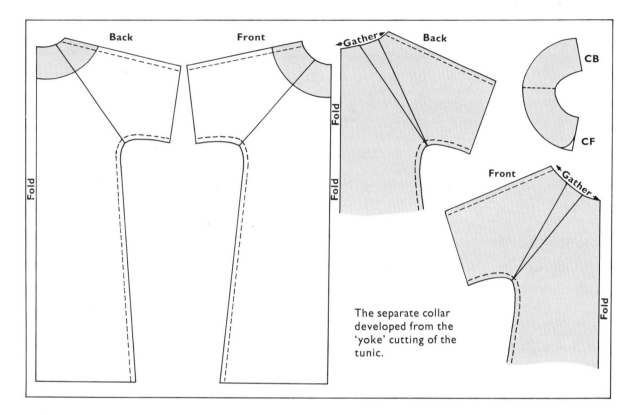

Back   Front   ◄ Gather   Back

Fold   Fold   CB   CF

Fold   Front   Gather ►   Fold

The separate collar developed from the 'yoke' cutting of the tunic.

The Magyar sleeve was a further development in the jig-saw tunic. Jewelled yokes were a sign of wealth, and the separate collar could be changed from garment to garment.

Cutting down the Magyar line and 'spreading' the neckline, without altering the side seam, allowed for the neckline to be gathered into the peasant blouse, still worn today.

THE OVER-TUNIC AND THE COTE

Super- or over-tunics began to be worn over the basic tunic. Usually heavily trimmed to increase the weight at the hem which helped it to hang well, the over-tunic would be split to below the waist, displaying the under tunic. The semicircular roman toga was modified to form the cape, thrown over and around the shoulders, and caught to one side with a clasp.

Sleeves were set into a deep armhole, and the curved sides created a closer fit. Slits were left in the side seams to allow the wearer to get to the money pouch, which would be attached to the girdle or belt.

The over-tunic eventually became the 'cote' of the thirteenth century.

Clasps like this Frankish sixth-century silver and miello brooch, were both useful and attractive.

The closer fitting woman's tunic also used lacing to fasten the back seam.

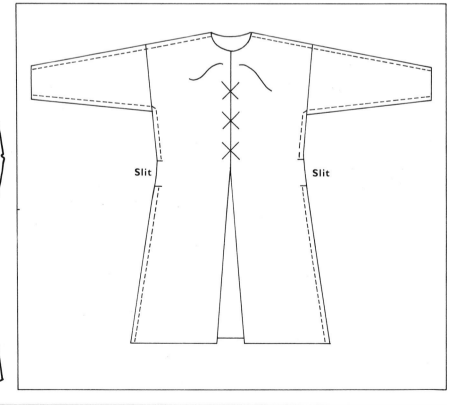

Slit

Slit

BREECHES

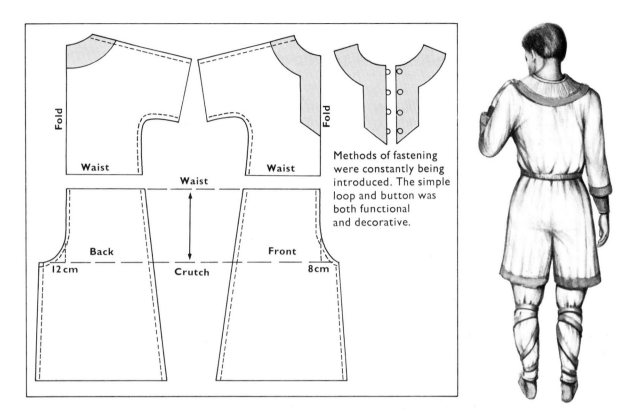

Methods of fastening were constantly being introduced. The simple loop and button was both functional and decorative.

The introduction of the divided skirt-tunic came with the Norman conquest of Britain in 1066. Worn by the conquerors it represented the first simple short trousers, and also became the first predominantly male garment.

The divided skirt could be joined at the waist, to the bodice, but would more likely be a separate garment with a cord gathering the waist to fit. The waistband was a later development.

INTRODUCING THE WAISTLINE

Once the breeches or divided skirt came into fashion for male garments, creating a two-piece outfit, it brought about a more defined waist emphasis in women's garments.

The tunic top was retained, often with a decorative undersleeve, but the skirt was cut separately and in many styles.

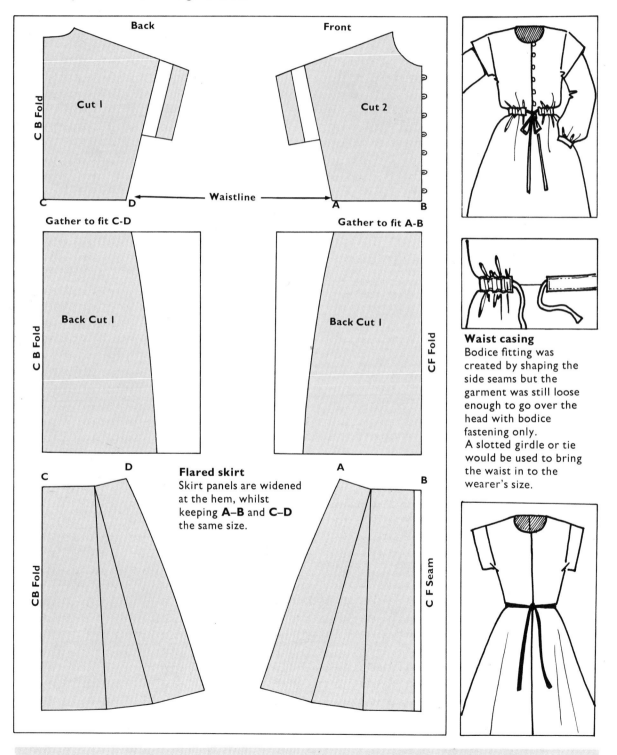

Back

Front

C B Fold

Cut 1

Cut 2

C   D   Waistline   A   B

Gather to fit C-D

Gather to fit A-B

C B Fold

Back Cut 1

Back Cut 1

CF Fold

Flared skirt
Skirt panels are widened at the hem, whilst keeping **A–B** and **C–D** the same size.

C   D

A   B

CB Fold

C F Seam

Waist casing
Bodice fitting was created by shaping the side seams but the garment was still loose enough to go over the head with bodice fastening only.
A slotted girdle or tie would be used to bring the waist in to the wearer's size.

TAKING SHAPE

The hang of the skirt was important, and by trial and error, it became obvious that the four-piece skirt looked and hung better if the straight warp threads went down the centre of the panel. The closer body fitting for both male and female dress started with the bodice. Shaping in the side seams emphasised the waist, to which a variety of skirts could be attached.

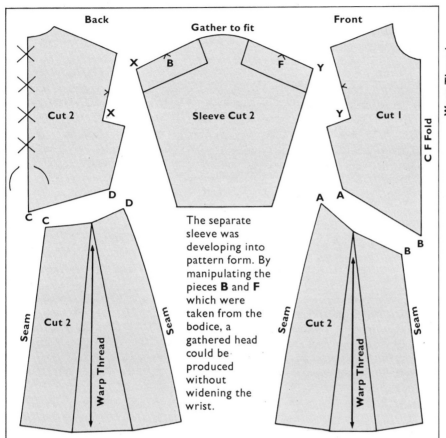

The separate sleeve was developing into pattern form. By manipulating the pieces **B** and **F** which were taken from the bodice, a gathered head could be produced without widening the wrist.

In woven cloth the vertical threads are known as the warp and the horizontal ones as the weft. On the loom the warp threads are first laid lengthwise and cross-woven with the weft threads. In modern dressmaking the warp threads are called the 'grain' of the fabric.

Lacing tightened the fit and closed the garment.

SEAM SHAPING

Still working from the basic tunic outline, designers saw the possibility of making a garment fit more closely by using seaming to bring a fabric into the shape of the body. A larger number of small pieces of fabric could be used to create both fit and added interest. The armhole followed more closely the line of the body and armpit, which allowed for maximum arm movement.

Although the pattern can be clearly seen as a jig-saw it must be remembered that when a garment pattern is cut up, it must have a seam allowance added to allow it to be sewn together again.

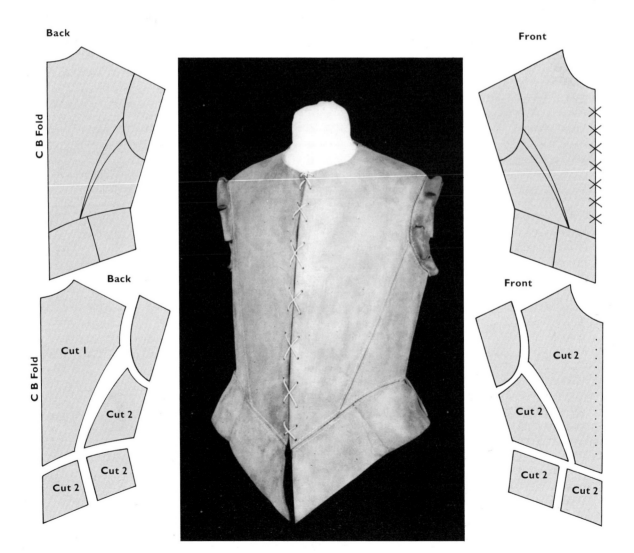

NECKLINE CHANGES

Seam shaping was to play an important part in the emphasis of the female figure. Lower necklines added feminity to garments, and most bodices were fully lined so that no raw edges were seen. Full gathered skirts would complete the gown.

VERTICAL SHAPING

Fitting flat fabric closer to the body became a feature of changing fashions, both for male and female costume. Vertical cutting allowed the fabric to be contoured to the body, and produced what is now called 'in-seam' shaping.

The circumference of the bust (or chest) was reduced at the waist to the waist circumference and out again to the hip circumference, by shaping the seam-lines both at the front and back of a garment.

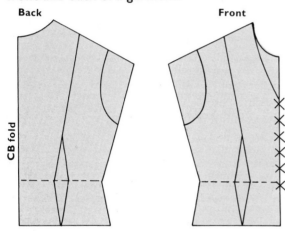

Back   Front

CB fold

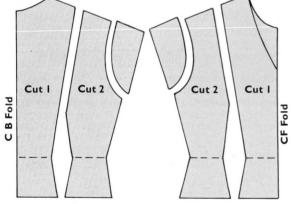

C B Fold   Cut I   Cut 2   Cut 2   Cut I   CF Fold

Close fitting meant more careful cutting, and it must always be remembered that if the pieces are to be sewn together again a seam allowance must be added to the cut edges.

CONTROLLING THE FIGURE

As it became fashionable to fit garments closer,
so it became the fashion to control the body
shape underneath. Laced and boned undergarments created the shape that the fashion of
the day dictated and the design of undergarments was to play a vital part in the evolution of female dress through the centuries. The
fashionable fitted waist, dipping to a low 'V' on
the skirt, which emphasised the waist and
flattened the bust, was created by stiff boning
of the fabric and by lacing both front and back
of the bodice.

CONTROLLING THE FIGURE

A complete industry was evolved to make corsets and undergarments which led to the huge companies of today creating bras and foundation garments. The shape of women's fashion since the sixteenth century has depended to a large extent on the corsets, padding, bustles, and crinolines that changed a woman's natural outline to that of the designers choosing.

Several layers of undergarments were worn in the 19th and early 20th centuries. Corsets pulled the waist in and the bust out, a crinoline held the skirt out and padding emphasized the hip line.

The 1850s saw a time of affluence which was mirrored in the fashion world by bigger and bigger skirts. These became so heavy that whalebone or steel crinolines were needed to hold them up.

DRESSMAKING
WITH PATTERNS

Towards the middle of the nineteenth century changes in fashion were becoming more frequent. The advent of the lock-stitch sewing machine, invented by Elias Howe in 1864, saw the dawn of a new era in the dressmaking and tailoring field. The lock-stitch machine was in mass production, and being widely used, by 1865, and, as the sewing processes speeded up so the shapes and pieces that made up a garment became more complex. Magazines for women began to be available and they displayed the latest styles, which the dressmakers and tailors were asked to copy for their clients. Dressmakers' dummies became popular, individually made for customers, so that designs could be created by draping calico or mull onto the standing dummy. The seams and shaping could be marked, and the resulting **toile** or fabric pattern would then be unpicked so that a flat pattern could be copied from it. This method is still widely used by couture dressmakers, and early descriptions of this way of working can be found in a *Book of Trades* dated 1804.

From the early nineteenth century, patterns were also being produced by 'scientific methods' based on the natural proportions of the body and mathematical calculations; this method is also widely used today and is known as flat-pattern drafting. By the end of the nineteenth century factories were producing moderately priced ready-to-wear clothes for the middle and lower classes to buy. Home-dressmaking began to flourish, copying the ready-to-wear styles and using patterns which were included in magazines both in Britain, Europe and America.

The big pattern companies came into being in America where the sewing machine for domestic use was first mass produced. The Butterick Company was founded in 1863 by Ebenezer Butterick of Massachusetts, followed in 1870 by the McCall Company, founded by a Scotsman, James McCall who lived in New York. By 1876 Butterick had offices in London, Paris, Berlin and Vienna, and, together with McCalls and other companies such as Simplicity, Vogue (part of Butterick), and Style (part of Simplicity) they have continued to dominate the pattern field for the home dressmaker to this day. All the pattern companies base their patterns on Standard Size Body Measurements. They are very accurate, and meticulously produced, and there would be no problem at all for the home dressmaker today if we had standard size people – but we don't, and that is where the problems begin.

NEW EQUIPMENT FOR A NEW ERA

The pattern companies have Master Patterns _ their basic blocks for standard size ranges _ and they know how to adapt these blocks to create each new style. Pattern adaption is not difficult to learn, it requires a logical mind, and some basic arithmetic, and the ability to draw straight and curved lines. A straight ruler and a dressmakers curved ruler will even make that easier to do. Artistic ability is an added bonus, but some of the best pattern-makers in the world cannot sketch. However, the connection between the sort of draftsmanship required in both engineering and pattern-cutting has proved very helpful when a friend who is an engineer can be brought in on the job.

The correct beginning for your dressmaking must therefore be a Master Pattern that fits. The following pages give you detailed instruction on how to measure, and how to translate those measurements into a Master Pattern.

STAGE 1 MEASURING

Taking your measurements

It is impossible to take your own measurements, and you will need the assistance of someone else to ensure accuracy. Measurements are best taken over a fitted garment, with set in sleeves, to that the contours of your body can be clearly seen. A piece of tape should be firmly tied around your waist to position your waistline accurately. Care must be taken to allow the tight tape to settle where your waistline actually is – which is not always where you would like it to be. Follow the measuring instructions carefully and write in each step as you go, in the 'boxes' provided.

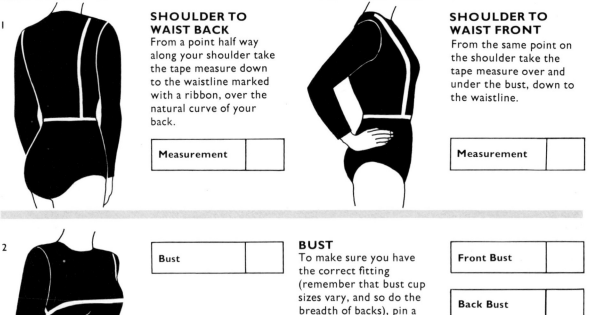

1

SHOULDER TO WAIST BACK
From a point half way along your shoulder take the tape measure down to the waistline marked with a ribbon, over the natural curve of your back.

Measurement	

SHOULDER TO WAIST FRONT
From the same point on the shoulder take the tape measure over and under the bust, down to the waistline.

Measurement	

2

Bust	

BUST
To make sure you have the correct fitting (remember that bust cup sizes vary, and so do the breadth of backs), pin a piece of tape from bustline to waistline under each arm at the side seams. Now measure the front and back halves of your body.

Front Bust	

Back Bust	

3

BUST DARTS POSITION
This is a crucial body fitting, and one essential to all dress design, as you will see later on. Get it wrong and your whole garment will be a disaster. First find out how high your bust is. Measure up from the waist to the point of the bust with a ruler.

Bust Height	

PREPARING THE PAPER RECTANGLES

Lines **A–B** are drawn 2.5cm down from the top edge. All horizontal lines are pencilled to line **A–B**. **Prepare the front first**.

Transfer letters **A**, **B** etc. to the inside edges of your rectangle, so that you will have them on the rectangle when it is cut.

BACK

B–C = **B–C** on Front	**J–L** = 12.5cm
B–E = **B–E** on Front	**L–N** = 5cm
E–G = 5cm	**N–P** = 17.5cm

FRONT

B–E = ½ **B–J**	**J–L** = 12.5cm
B–C = ½ **B–E**	**L–N** = 5cm
G–J = Bust Height	**N–P** = 17.5cm

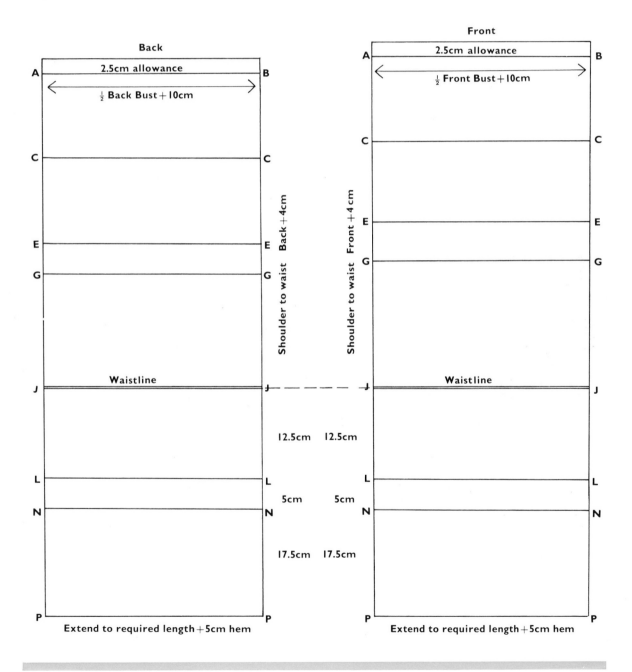

Back

A — 2.5cm allowance — B
½ Back Bust+10cm

Shoulder to waist Back+4cm

Waistline

12.5cm 12.5cm

5cm 5cm

17.5cm 17.5cm

Extend to required length+5cm hem

Front

A — 2.5cm allowance — B
½ Front Bust+10cm

Shoulder to waist Front+4cm

Waistline

Extend to required length+5cm hem

WAIST

Take this measurement (not too tightly) where your waist tape has settled.

HIPS

Take two hip measurements (three for the fuller hip).

1st Hip	
2nd Hip	
3rd Hip	

SHOULDER WIDTH

Measure across your back, noting where the sleeve is set in on the fitted garment you are wearing, and checking if this is where you prefer it to be.

½ Shoulder width + 1.5cm dart	

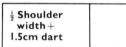

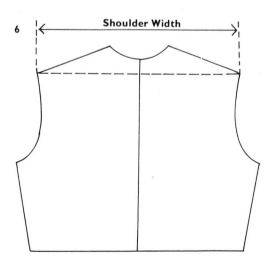

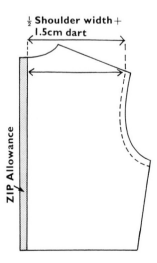

PLOTTING THE PATTERN

Using the measurements I–6, and carefully following the detailed instructions on each line, plot your measurements onto the front and back, rectangles. Use a green felt-tip pen and a dashed line to join up the points marked.

A dressmaker's 'French curved ruler' would help you to draw curves. The point **Z** is dividing the shoulder in half.
Extend to required skirt length + 5cm hem.

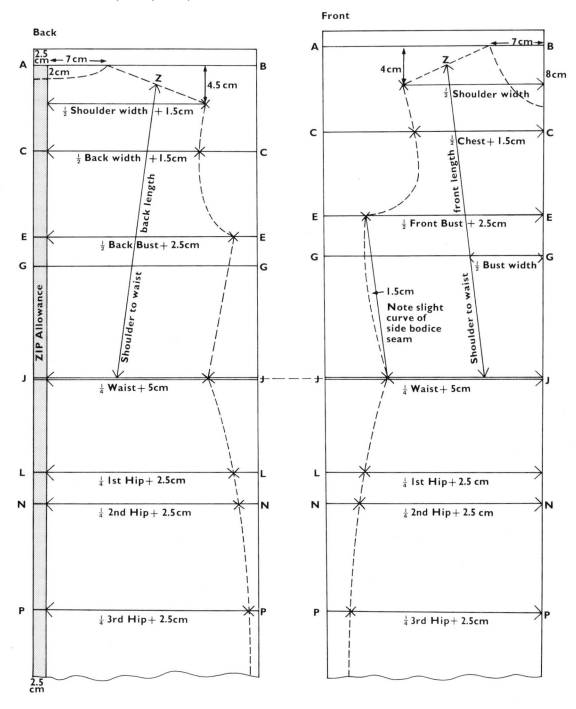

Back

- A 2.5 cm — 7 cm →   B
- 2cm
- Z
- 4.5 cm
- ½ Shoulder width + 1.5cm
- C   ½ Back width + 1.5cm   C
- back length
- E   ½ Back Bust + 2.5cm   E
- G   G
- ZIP Allowance
- Shoulder to waist
- J   ¼ Waist + 5cm   J
- L   ¼ 1st Hip + 2.5cm   L
- N   ¼ 2nd Hip + 2.5cm   N
- P   ¼ 3rd Hip + 2.5cm   P
- 2.5 cm

Front

- A   7 cm →   B
- 4 cm   Z   8cm
- ½ Shoulder width
- C   ½ Chest + 1.5cm   C
- front length
- E   ½ Front Bust + 2.5cm   E
- G   ½ Bust width   G
- 1.5cm
- Note slight curve of side bodice seam
- Shoulder to waist
- J   ¼ Waist + 5cm   J
- L   ¼ 1st Hip + 2.5 cm   L
- N   ¼ 2nd Hip + 2.5 cm   N
- P   ¼ 3rd Hip + 2.5cm   P

35

ADDING THE DETAIL

1 Cut round the front and back pattern leaving a 1.5cm seam allowance on the edges as indicated.

2 Point **Z** is midway between **A–B** on back shoulder, and **C–D** on front shoulder.

BACK
Point **R** is midway between **P–Q**. Join **Z–R** and continue line to point **X** on waist line. Complete the waist dart as indicated.

FRONT
Point **Z** is midway between **C–D**. Point **R** is making half the bust width. Join **Z** to **R** and continue to **X** on the waistline. Complete the waist dart as indicated.

3 SIDE BUST DART
Place the waistline of the front and back patterns level. The front side bodice seam will be *longer* than the back side bodice seam.
Measure the difference **A–B**.
Measure this different down from **C** to point **D** on the front bodice. Join **D** to **R** to complete the correct side bust dart.

4 BACK SHOULDER DART
From point **Z** measure 1.5cm to point **F**. Draw line from **F** to **H** to complete the back shoulder dart.

ADDING THE DETAIL

Place front and back with waistlines level. Measure **A–B**. Measure **C–D** = **A–B**. Draw in front side-bust dart.

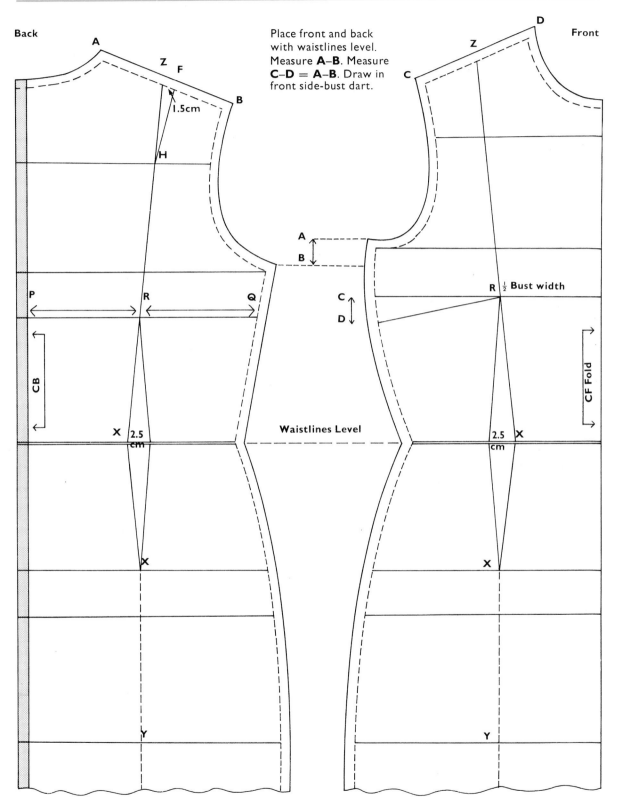

BACK FOR ROUND SHOULDERS

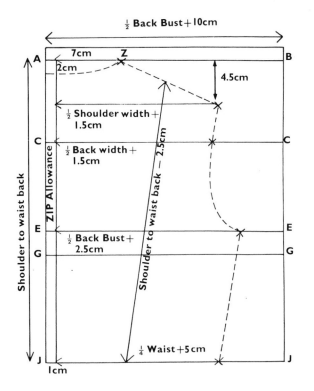

½ Back Bust+10cm

7cm

Z

2cm

B

A

4.5cm

½ Shoulder width + 1.5cm

Shoulder to waist back − 2.5cm

C — C

½ Back width + 1.5cm

ZIP Allowance

Shoulder to waist back

E — E

½ Back Bust+ 2.5cm

G — G

¼ Waist+5cm

J — J

1cm

Prepare rectangle as for normal stance except that line **A–J** = shoulder to waist back measurement, only with no addition.

Note: The shoulder to waist back line will be the actual measurement minus 2.5cm.

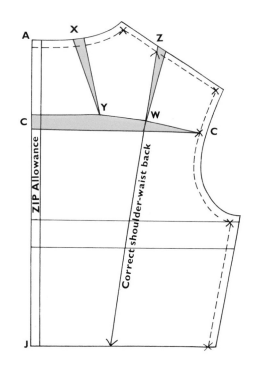

A

X

Z

Y

W

C

C

ZIP Allowance

Correct shoulder-waist back

J

TO CORRECT THE BACK

Cut around the pattern leaving 1.6cm lining as indicated. Cut along the lines **C–C**, **X–Z**, **Y–W** and spread the upper pattern until the shoulder to waist back measurement is correct. Keep the back line **A–J** straight.

This will give an extra neck dart and also increases the shoulder dart.

BACK FOR SLOPING STANCE

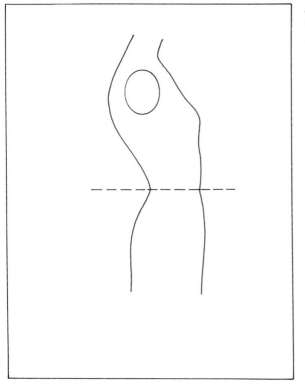

A sloping stance gives an elongated shoulder to waist back measurement which is very different from round shoulders.

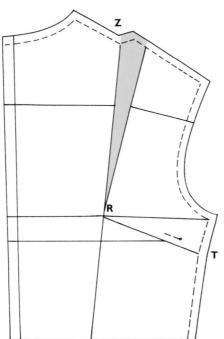

TO CORRECT THE BACK PATTERN

Prepare the block exactly as for normal stance. Cut around the pattern leaving 1.6cm turning as indicated. Cut down line **Z–R** and fold out a 1.3cm dart at point **T** finishing at point **R**. This will increase the shoulder dart. Careful use of styling, particularly yokes and princess line garments, will disguise this problem.

BASIC SLEEVE BLOCK

Pin the front and back pattern together at the shoulder seam. Measure the arm stitching line from armhole.

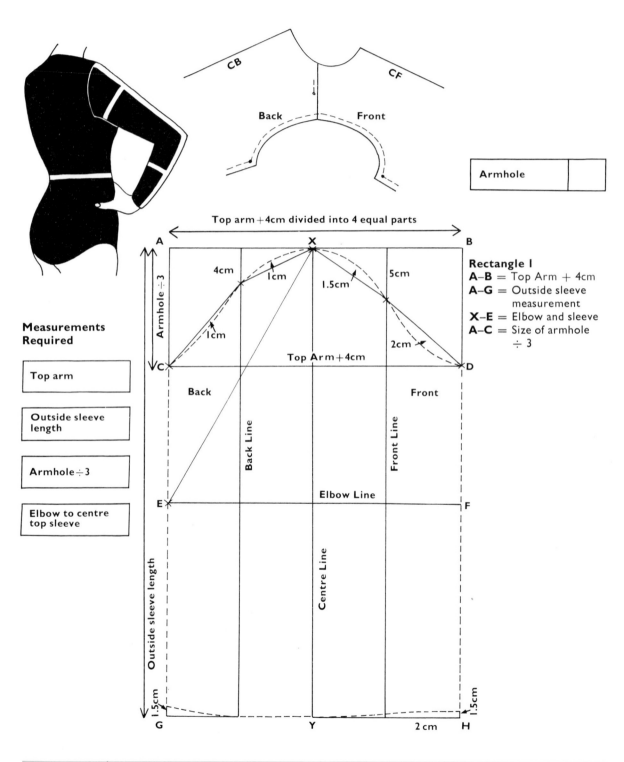

Armhole	

Measurements Required

Top arm

Outside sleeve length

Armhole ÷ 3

Elbow to centre top sleeve

Top arm + 4cm divided into 4 equal parts

Armhole ÷ 3

Top Arm + 4cm

4cm   1cm   1.5cm   5cm

1cm   2cm

Back   Front

Back Line   Front Line

Elbow Line

Centre Line

Outside sleeve length

1.5cm   1.5cm

G   Y   2 cm   H

Rectangle I
A–B = Top Arm + 4cm
A–G = Outside sleeve measurement
X–E = Elbow and sleeve
A–C = Size of armhole ÷ 3

FINISHED SLEEVE

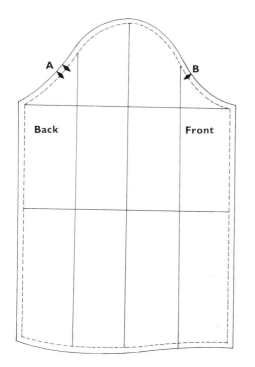

FINISHED SLEEVE

Cut out the sleeve, allowing a 1.6cm seam on all edges. Place balance notches on front and back at **A** and **B**.

Note: Gathering line between **A–B** to ease sleeve into armhole.

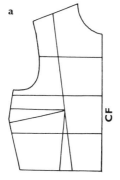

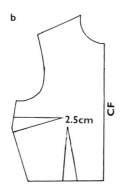

MAKING UP THE MASTER PATTERN

1 Stitch centre back seam up to approximately 15cm below waist, and insert zip.
2 Stitch all darts and press.
3 Stitch shoulder seams.
4 Add neck facings
5 Insert sleeves, on the flat OR bind armholes.
6 Stitch side seams and sleeves seams in one operation.
7 Adjust hems and hand stitch.

Darts on the Master Pattern

a) For the purpose of dress design and adaptation the front waist darts and the side bust dart are shown to be touching each other.

b) In practice if you were machining the darts in this position they must not meet. The side bust dart should finish 2.5cm away from the dart coming up from the waist, as illustrated.

TROUSER BLOCK INSTRUCTIONS

Place the skirt blocks, front and back, with side seams touching and draw round them down to the crutch depth, **A–B**. Omit back zip allowance. Draw line **H–K** at the crutch depth **A–B**. Extend **H** by 10cm to **D** (add 0.2cm for every 4cm hip increase over 102cm).
Extend **K** by 7.5cm to **G** (add 0.2cm for every 4cm hip increase over 102cm).

CRUTCH CURVE
Draw the front and back curves as indicated.
Note: The centre back waistline is raised by 2cm to point **X**. The centre back waist is reduced by 1cm to point **R**. The back dart is reduced by 1cm to compensate.

WAISTLINE
The raised **CB** waist lowers to 1cm above natural waistline at the side seams and lowers to the natural waistline at **CF**.

CREASELINES
Front: Point $F = \frac{1}{2}$ **B–G**.
Back: **B–E** = **B–F**.
Note: Point **E** is not midway between **D–B**.

TROUSER LENGTH
A–C = Side leg measurement.

TROUSER WIDTH
The width varies at knee and ankle as fashions change. Average measurements are as indicated on the diagram.

CRUTCH MEASUREMENT

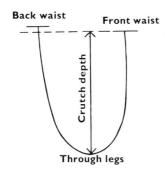

BASIC TROUSER BLOCK (Based on Skirt)

MEASUREMENTS REQUIRED

Crutch depth		Outside leg	

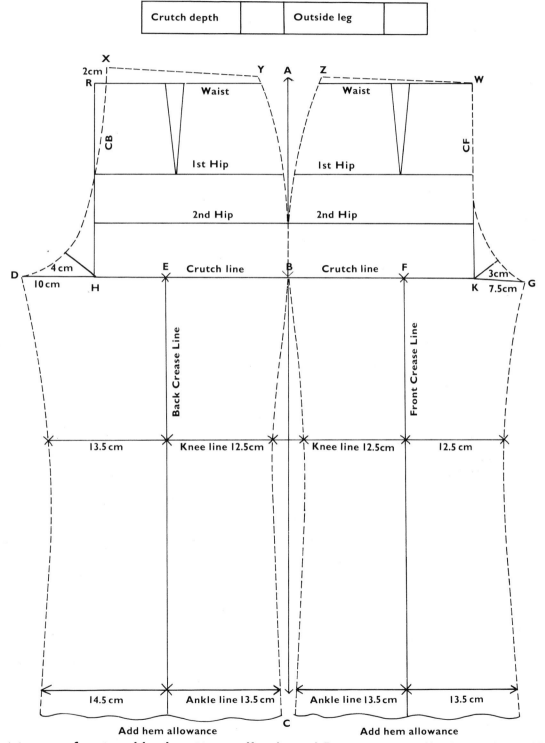

Cut trouser front and back pattern, allowing a 1.5cm seam on all edges. Note: Hem.

CREATING FASHION

All fabric is flat, and the advent of fitted clothes and the need to shape the fabric to the body has played a major part in the development of patterns for dressmaking. As more fitting was called for, vertical cutting lines were used to contour the garment to the figure, giving shaped seaming. With the introduction of paper patterns a new word appeared in the dressmaker's vocabulary – the dart. If you look at the vertical cutting on page 129 you can easily see that the contouring created by the seam line could have been created without cutting the fabric, but by stitching the dart shaped area which allows the material to go in from the bust to the waist and out again to the hips. Today these are called waist darts. In the Basic Master Pattern you will also see a side-bust dart. This dart is necessary to contour the fabric to the bust shape, and is very different, both in size and position, from person to person. There is also a back shoulder dart to allow the fabric to fit over the shoulder blades closely. Two simple processes have to be understood before you start to read the pattern adapting section of the book:

1. The Basic Master Pattern can be cut up – like a jig-saw puzzle both vertically and horizontally, to create a new outline.
You need to add seams to allow the pattern to be reassembled.

2. The side-bust dart in the Master Pattern can be moved around into any position.
If you think of the side-bust dart as being the slice taken out of a circular cake, you will see immediately that you can move the 'gap' caused by the removal of the slice into any position.

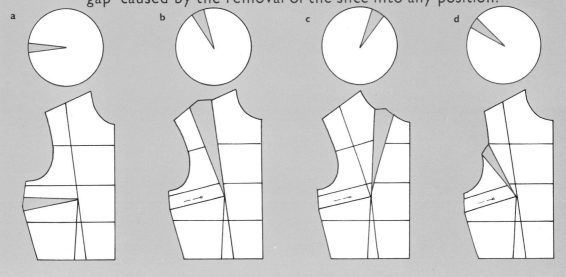

a   b   c   d

LOOKING AT THE BASIC PATTERN

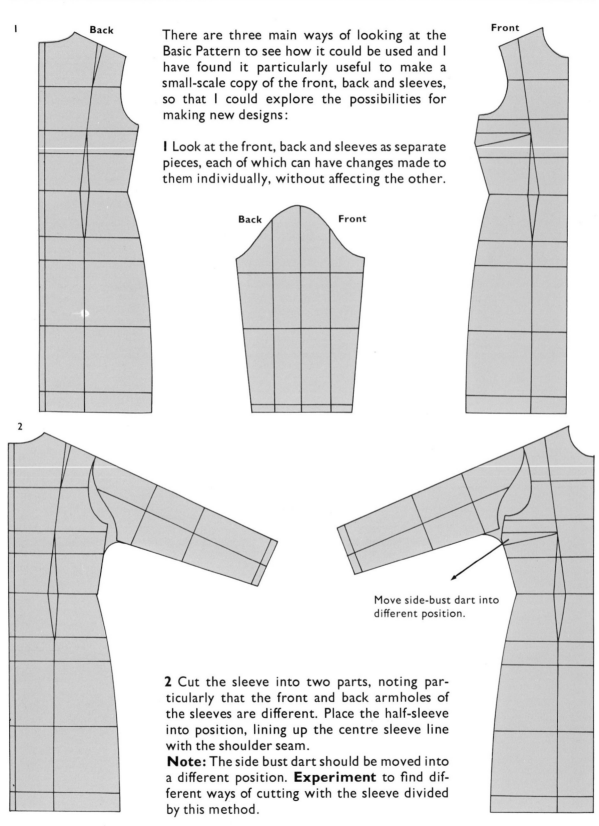

There are three main ways of looking at the Basic Pattern to see how it could be used and I have found it particularly useful to make a small-scale copy of the front, back and sleeves, so that I could explore the possibilities for making new designs:

1 Look at the front, back and sleeves as separate pieces, each of which can have changes made to them individually, without affecting the other.

Move side-bust dart into different position.

2 Cut the sleeve into two parts, noting particularly that the front and back armholes of the sleeves are different. Place the half-sleeve into position, lining up the centre sleeve line with the shoulder seam.
Note: The side bust dart should be moved into a different position. **Experiment** to find different ways of cutting with the sleeve divided by this method.

LOOKING AT THE BASIC PATTERN

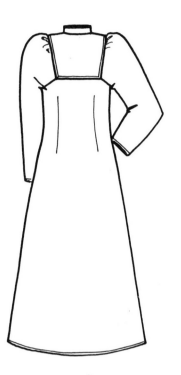

If you cut out the sleeves as **A–B–C–D**, you can spread the top **B–C** gather it up to fit, and sew the sleeve back into position.

Gather

B   C

A   D

3

B

A

C

D

Move side-bust dart into different position.

3 Place the shoulders of the Master Pattern together then line up the complete sleeve with the shoulder seam and centre sleeve level.
Note: Again the side-bust dart would be better moved to a different position.

Experiment with the pattern in this form to see what ideas for design you can create.

SLEEVES

The introduction of the separately-cut sleeve brought a new dimension to the making of clothes. The sleeve became a focal point for changes in style. Slim fitting and cut on the bias of the fabric, full gathers at the sleeve head, wide loose sleeve, sleeves gathered into the wrist, pads to make the sleeve lift at the shoulder . . . the list of possibilities is endless and designers use this feature to the full. The sleeve can be in a different fabric to the rest of the garment. Expensive and elaborate embroidery can be featured, either on the sleeve itself, or on the cuff. The variety of cuffs that can be used will change the whole look of a sleeve. Two sleeves can be used together, giving a top sleeve and under sleeve, with both being stitched together into the armhole, the undersleeve often in a light delicate fabric, with a heavier oversleeve cut from the same fabric as the main garment. The position in which the sleeve is stitched to the bodice, often changes the style. Dropped shoulder lines, raised shoulder lines, the use of exaggerated shoulder pads all are part of the history of fashion. When you add the kimono (magyar) and raglan and dolman sleeve variations, you can well see how the simple sleeve can dictate today's changes of fashion.

SLEEVES

PUFF SLEEVE

The puff sleeve is created by cutting the basic sleeve to the required length, then cutting through the three vertical lines on the pattern and spreading both top and bottom of the sleeve to produce the required fullness.

FITTED SLEEVE

Slim sleeves which fit the arm are created by first reducing the sides of the basic pattern, tapering towards the wrist, leaving the sleeve head intact, then cutting from the back edge to the centre line, folding a dart out from the bottom, to bring the sleeve to the required wrist measurement.

BISHOP SLEEVE

Bishop sleeves normally fit smoothly into the sleeve armhole, with gathered fullness going into a cuff or wrist band. The pattern is cut up the three vertical lines and spread to any measurement. The cuff opening is always on the back arm line, and the sleeve can be cut with a rise at the bottom front line.

CAPE SLEEVE

The cape effect is created because of the circular cutting of the sleeve bottom. Cut the sleeve up the three vertical lines, then select the length required, then cut up the three vertical lines spreading the bottom until the sleeve head is almost straight.

SLEEVES

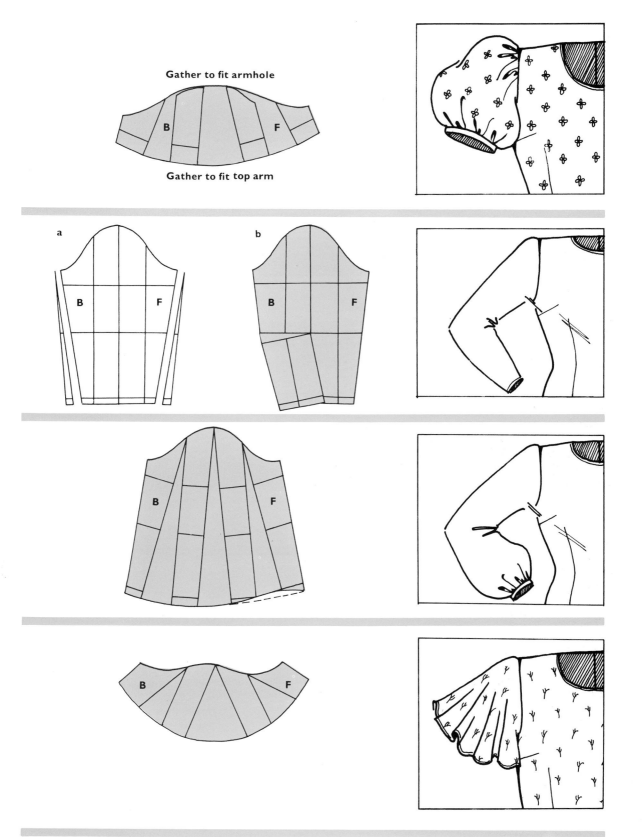

Gather to fit armhole

B

F

Gather to fit top arm

a

B F

b

B F

B F

B F

SLEEVES

The idea of combining two sleeves to create style is part of costume history. The lighter fabric used for the gathered undersleeve is very effective with a heavier contrast oversleeve.

GATHERED SLEEVE

The gathered sleeve is created by cutting up the three vertical lines on the pattern and spreading the sleeve both at the sleeve head and at the bottom. The amount of gather required governs the amount of spread required. The sleeve is finished at the bottom either by a cuff, wristband, cord slotted through to tie, or by elastication.

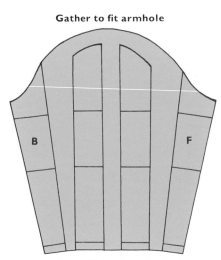

Gather to fit armhole

B   F

Gather to fit cuff or elasticate

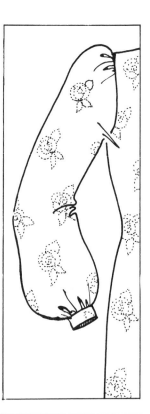

OVER SLEEVE

a) Cut through the vertical line on the front of the sleeve, and place the piece removed into position as indicated. The bottom line **F–G** can be spread to any width required.

b) The new sleeve fits smoothly into the armhole, and the straight grain (the warp) of the fabric should be noted.

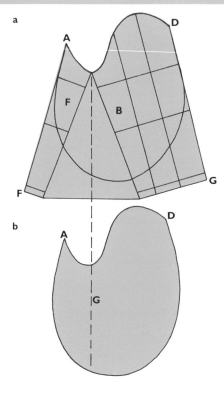

a

A   D

F   B

F   G

b

A   D

G

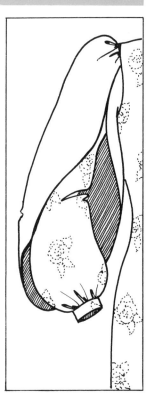

SLEEVES

SIMPLE TWO-PIECE SLEEVES

Cutting the sleeve into two sections can be useful, not only because it creates new styles but because it can often be the means of using fabric more economically.

1 The sleeve is cut down the centre line forming a front and back section. The cut edges can be neatened or bound with contrasting fabric, then caught at intervals to form a sleeve reminiscent of the Greek *chiton*.

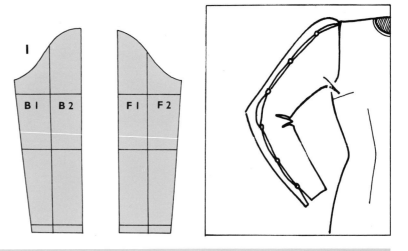

2 Separating the **BI** section from the rest of the sleeve gives a good line on which cuff detail can be correctly placed. It is also useful because this is the position for leaving the sleeve bottom opening for addition of cuffs or wristband which will fasten in to the actual wrist-size.

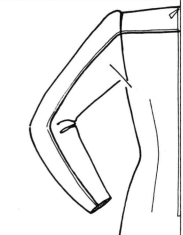

3 Section **BI** and **F2** are separated from the rest of the sleeve and are then placed together to form a new underarm section.

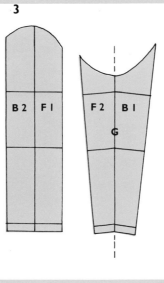

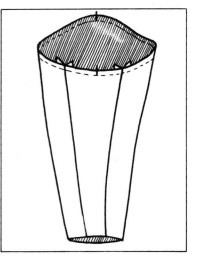

SLEEVES

TWO-PIECE SHAPED SLEEVE

a) The two-piece shaped sleeve is used mainly for jackets and more tailored garments. The starting point is to narrow the wrist slightly by trimming the side seams as indicated. Next cut through the middle line commencing on the back edge, and spread the sleeve pattern by 2.5cm.

b) Cut the sides from the front and back-sleeve and reposition them for the new underarm pattern piece, so that lines **A–D** and **X–Y** are equal on both the front and back edges.

c) With seams added, pieces **A–D** will be stitched together, followed by **X–Y** with seams added.

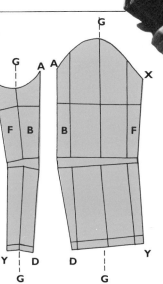

SLEEVES

FITTED SLEEVE: WITH GATHERED SLEEVE HEAD

The fitted sleeve, with a gathered sleeve head starts with the fitted sleeve pattern. The head is then cut down to line **X–Y** and the sections **F1**, **F2**, **B1** and **B2** repositioned with a 2.5cm gap in the centre of line **X–Y**. This gives the gathering ease at the head. This has, in fact, lengthened the sleeve. In order to emphasise the gathering, and also to retain the original length a 'sausage roll' shoulder pad will be needed. This will be stitched to the shoulder seam.

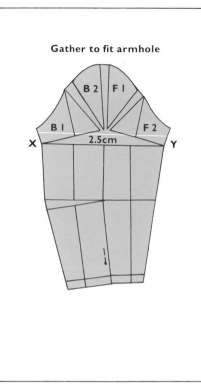

Gather to fit armhole

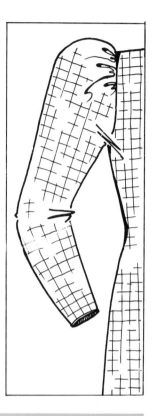

THE LEG OF MUTTON SLEEVE

The leg of mutton sleeve, so called because of the wide top, changing to a close fit towards the wrist has appeared many times in the history of costume. To be successful it requires an under-sleeve, **B1**, **B2**, **F1** and **F2**, which could be in lining fabric. This top sleeve pattern is then spread to form the gathering, both where it goes into the armhole and where it joins the fitted bottom sleeve. The top sleeve can be cut either on the straight grain of the fabric or, more successfully, on the direct cross-grain.

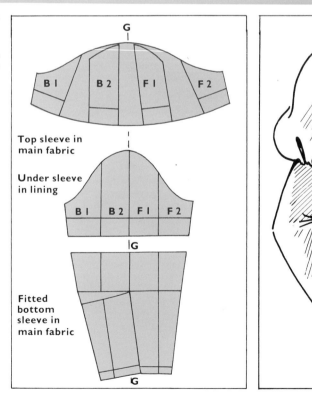

Top sleeve in main fabric

Under sleeve in lining

Fitted bottom sleeve in main fabric

SLEEVES

Sausage roll shoulder pad

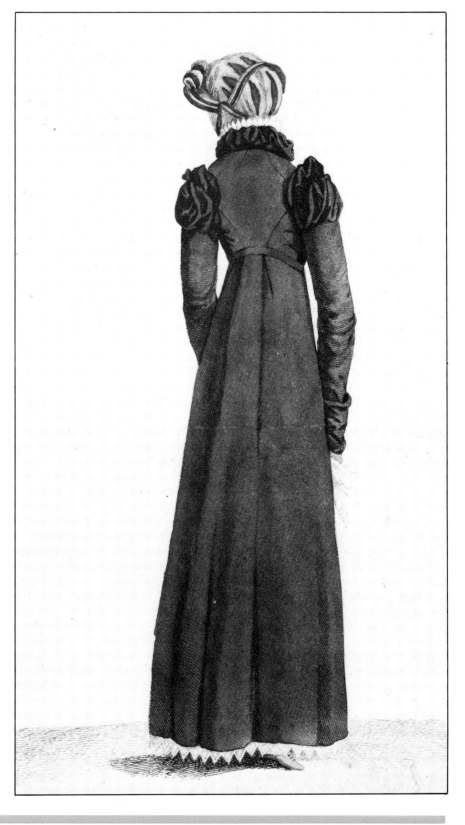

SLEEVES

FULL SLEEVE: FITTED FROM ELBOW TO WRIST

An extension of the leg-of-mutton sleeve was to increase the amount of gathering and fullness at the top, whilst retaining the fit at the elbow and wrist.

a) The fitted sleeve base was used and the sleeve was cut from point **A** to point **X** (approximately 10cm).

b) The sleeve head was then cut, and spread, as indicated, giving considerable gathering before the sleeve could be set into the armhole. To retain the gather at the top of the arm the sleeve head should be interfaced.

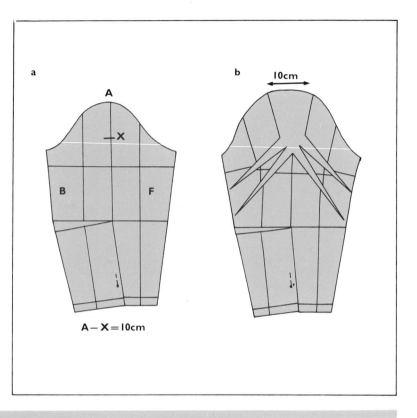

A — X = 10cm

FULL SLEEVE WITH FITTED HEAD AND NARROW WRIST BAND

This is a beautiful sleeve, most used in delicate, yet firm fabric such as organdie. The point where the bottom and top sleeve are stitched together could be trimmed or embroidered.

a) The basic sleeve is cut into a top and bottom section.

b) The top sleeve is cut and spread as indicated. Where the sleeve is spread, the sleeve should be dropped approximately 2.5cm between sections **BI** and **FI**.
The bottom sleeve is spread to match the top sleeve. To allow the hand to go through a back opening may be necessary, before a narrow wrist band is attached.

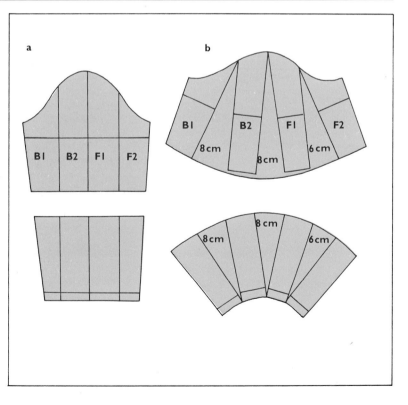

SLEEVES

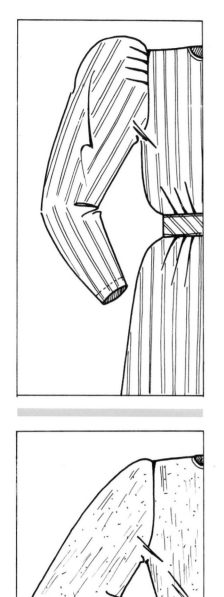

THE BODICE YOKE

1 The most simple form of yoke is when the front and back section of the bodice is separated from the remainder. This can be used very effectively in contrast fabric, and the stitching line, which rejoins the pieces can be top-stitched to add detail.

Note: The shoulder dart and shoulder seam are retained.

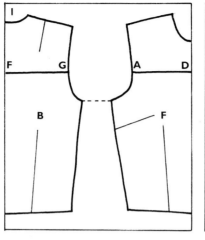

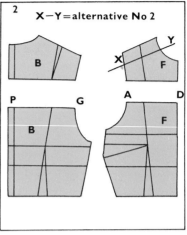

2, 2a The front yoke can be cut on the alternative **X–Y** line. This method is in general use for shirt manufacture. Front and back yokes are then placed together at the shoulder seam and cut as one piece. This does away with the shoulder seam. The side-bust dart can be moved into the yoke line, allowing either gathers or pleats to be used to bring **X–Y** on the bodice to equal **X–Y** on the yoke.

The waist darts should be changed to gathers to compliment the style.

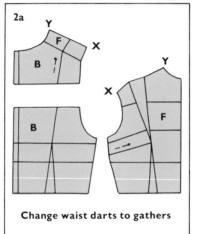

Change waist darts to gathers

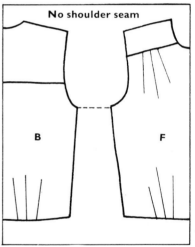

No shoulder seam

3 A yoke can be cut in any position or shape. A curved yoke on both front and back should balance in depth-of-cut from the shoulder into the armhole. The side-bust dart is moved into the yoke line and additional gathering can be achieved by spreading the pattern as illustrated. At the same time the side seams can be slightly flared.

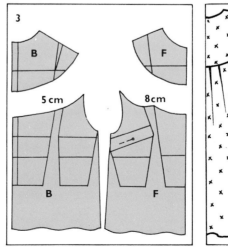

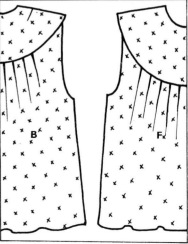

YOKE AND SLEEVES

COMBINING THE YOKE AND SLEEVES

a) The yoke pieces.

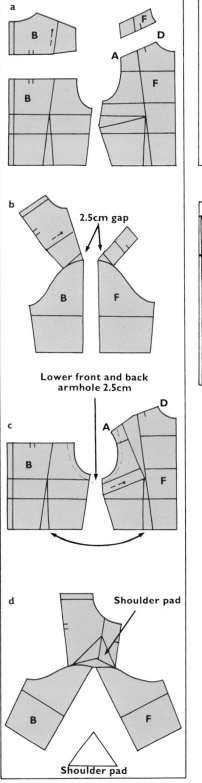

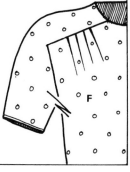

b) The sleeve is cut into two down the centre line, and yoke pieces are put into position with one edge touching the sleeve and the shoulder seam outer-edge of the yokes raised by 2.5cm forming the new pattern pieces for the front and back.

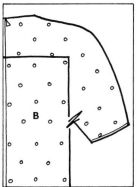

2.5cm gap

Lower front and back armhole 2.5cm

c) The side-bust dart is moved into the yoke position on line **A–D**. Gathers or pleats can be used to take this line **A–D** back to the original length. The front and back armholes are lowered by 2.5cm sufficient to allow the sleeve to stitch in without too much ease allowance. The waist darts should be used as gathers *or* they can be left unstitched allowing the garment to hang loosely at the waist.

d) A soft shoulder pad should be used to emphasise the natural shoulder of the garment.

Shoulder pad

Shoulder pad

SLEEVES

KIMONO SLEEVE AND DROPPED SHOULDER LINE

1 Bodice. Cut through the back waist dart and close the back shoulder dart. Cut through the front waist dart and close the side dart. Place shoulder seams together at the neck edge and 2.5cm apart at the armhole edge. **Sleeve.** Place sleeve into position in a straight line from **X–Y**. Overlap the sleeve head at the shoulder seam by 2.5cm. Draw lines **L–M** curving at the sleeve centre. Ensure that the curved seam-line **L–Z** on the back is equal to **M–T** on the front.

2 Cut through the line **X–Y** to form the new pattern pieces for front and back bodice. The increased waist darts can be gathered, or pleated back to the waist size. Alternatively, they can be left out to allow the garment to fall loosely from the underarm.

Note: The underseam can be cut in any curved shape, matching front and back exactly, to form a wider sleeve. It can shape into the waist to form the popular 'batwing' effect.

3 By cutting through the curved line **L–M**, and through the shoulder line **X–R** you can produce either **a)** a short sleeve top, or **b)** the kimono top, but with a stitching line where the sleeve is stitched into the bodice.

bi) The sleeve attached to the dropped shoulder line can be altered in many ways. Cut into four sections, with the line **L–M** and the wrist line spread to increase the width, the sleeve can be gathered back to a cuff or wristband.

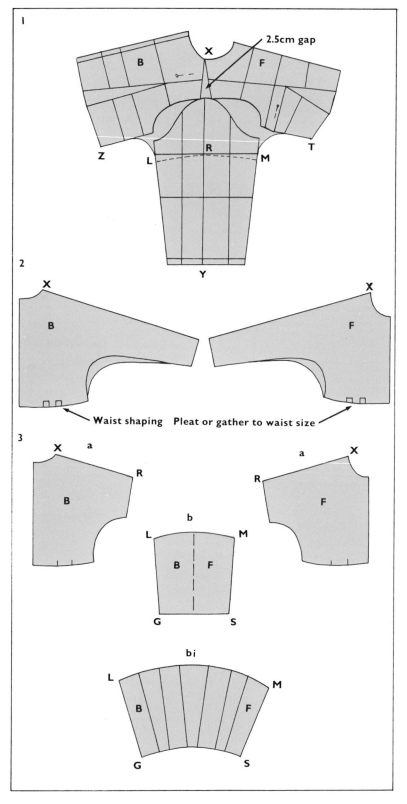

SLEEVES

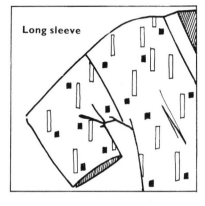

Long sleeve

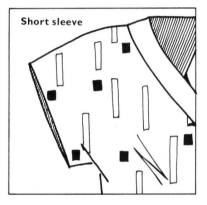

Short sleeve

SLEEVES

SIMPLE TWO-PIECE RAGLAN SLEEVE

a) The most simple raglan sleeve can be created by placing the front and back half of the sleeve into position with the front and back bodice, as indicated, keeping the shoulder seam and the sleeve seam in a straight line. This automatically drops the arm-hole, and the side-bust dart should be moved into a new position, in this case the neckline, where it can be used as gathers.

b) After drawing the curved lines **R–T** and **X–Y**, these are cut through to produce the new pattern pieces. Mark the notches where the sleeve fits back into the bodice front and back.

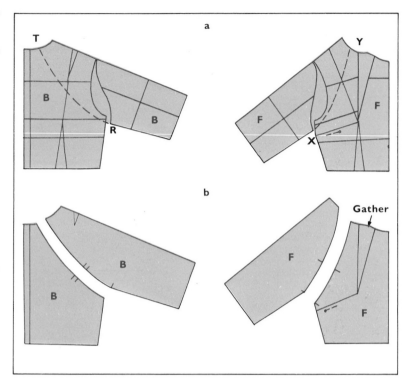

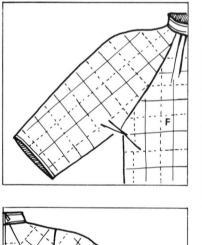

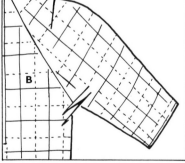

SLEEVES

ONE-PIECE RAGLAN SLEEVE

a) The one-piece raglan sleeve is formed by drawing the lines **R–T** and **X–Y** as indicated.

b) Take off the points left at **A** and **C** by drawing a smooth curve for **T–A–H** (back) and **Y–C–Z** (front).

c) Place the pieces cut from the bodice onto the sleeve head following the curve of the head. Draw smooth curves to form line **H–T** and **Y–Z** after closing out the shoulder dart on the back. This produces a one-piece raglan sleeve with a dart **A–C–D** forming the shoulder line when stitched.

d) The **A–C–D** dart can be partly, or completely, closed by first cutting up from **G** to **C** and then bringing point **A** to point **D**. The bottom of the sleeve can be left loose, gathered into a cuff or elasticated. This sleeve can be very effective when cut on the direct cross of the fabric. Other wise the line **C–G** remains the straight grain.

e) The cutting grain for the new sleeve is the line **C–G**. The lines **H–T** and **Z–Y** should be gently eased when stitched back to the bodice front and back.

f) This sleeve can also become a two-piece raglan – often used in jackets and coats. Cut up the line **C–G** and trim point **C** on each piece into a gentle curve. To widen the sleeve for the outer garment cut the pattern at points **H** and **Z** as indicated, and draw new underarm seam-line.

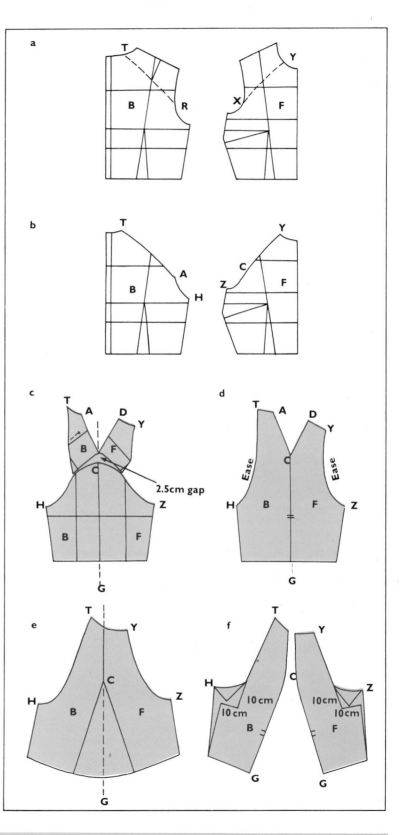

SLEEVES

WING SLEEVES WITH DEEP ARMHOLES

Place front and back bodice together at the shoulder seam. There is no need to close out the shoulder dart. Place the sleeve in position, keeping the centre sleeve in-line with the shoulder seam. Draw the new lines **A–X** and **D–Y** to connect with the sleeve underarm seams. Draw new line **A–D** to form sleeve head.

a) To allow for arm movement draw the curved lines **X–C** and **Y–H** making **A–X** and **D–Y** equal **A–X** and **D–Y** on the original **a)**.

b) Cut along these curved lines and lift and spread the pattern pieces as indicated in the diagram.

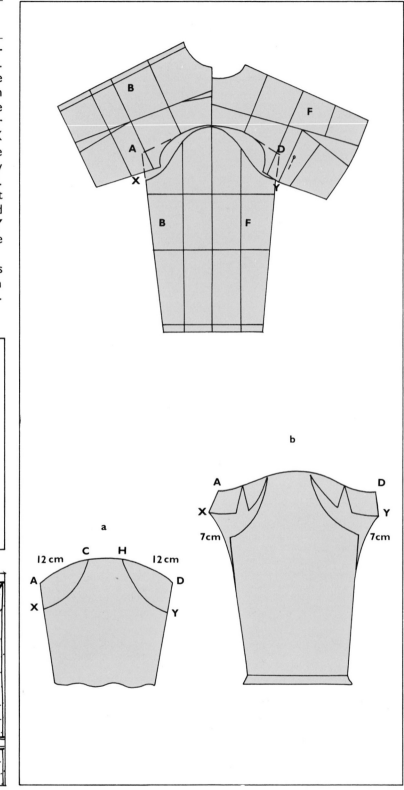

SLEEVES

c) The new pattern pieces can now be treated as normal front and back bodice, and normal sleeve. The sleeve can be spread to produce gathers at top or bottom, or both. The front and back bodice can be re-designed as required.

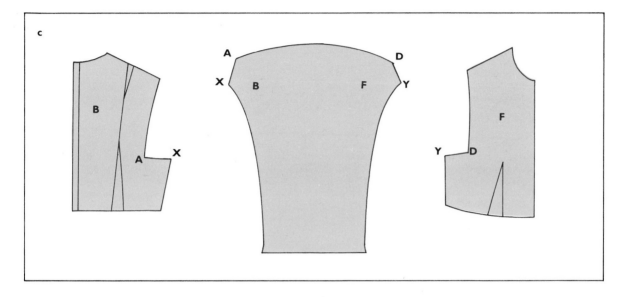

SLEEVES

DEEP ARMHOLE RAGLAN SLEEVE

a) Draw the lines **X–Y** on the back bodice, and **C–D** on the front bodice placing the points **C** and **Y** approximately 6cm down from the armhole. Cut through these lines, and place the cut-off pieces into position on the sleeve head, as indicated. This produces the new sleeve outline.

b) To lengthen the underarm seam and allow for arm movement, draw the lines **Y–R** and **C–S**.

bi) Cut round these lines and lift and spread the pieces as illustrated. Draw new curved underarm seams.

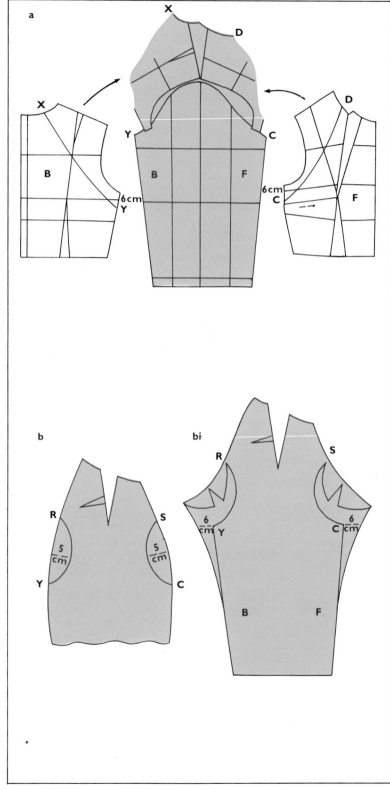

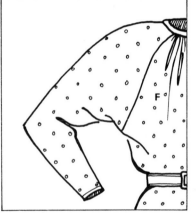

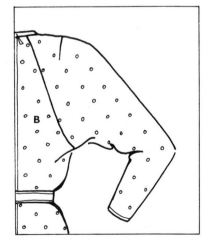

SLEEVES

DEEP ARMHOLE RAGLAN SLEEVE

c) The shoulder dart has been retained, but can be closed out at this stage, if preferred. Notches indicate where sleeve fits back to the bodice. The shoulder seam is created when the dart **X–Y–R** is stitched. The neckline and waistline darts can be used as gathers to take the pieces back to size.

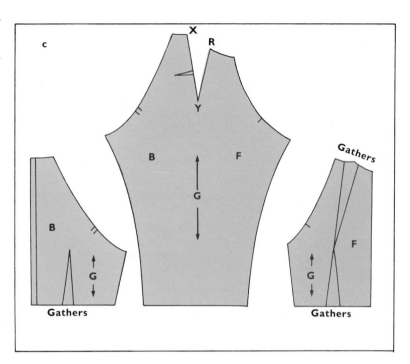

CAP SLEEVE

a) Draw the curved line on the sleeve head, using the measurements given.

b) Cut the sleeve on this line and spread the bottom until **A–D** is a straight line. This sleeve is best when cut to a fold at the bottom edge giving a complete sleeve facing. Alternatively the 'facing' or undersleeve can be in lining or contrast fabric.

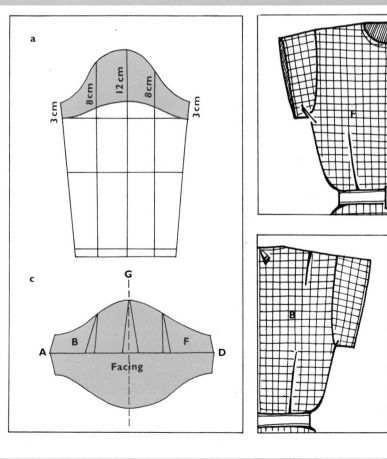

MISS ATHERTON·   MISS V·CAMERON·   MISS D·BROUGHTON·   MISS WILLIAMSON·

MISS BRANSCOMBE   MISS K·VAUGHAN·   MISS M·HOOD·

MISS GILCHRIST·   MISS GRUBBE·

MISS D'ANGELI·   MISS FARREN·   MISS PALMER·   MISS E·St·JOHN·

70

BODICES

The 'Female-Form-Divine' has looked very different down the ages wearing the fashionable clothes of the day. Sometimes well covered, sometimes cut low and revealing, with the bustline controlled by undergarments and corsetry, the bodice has always been the most difficult part of a garment to fit, because of the tremendous variation in women's sizes. The 'flat chested' look gave way to the voluptuous-curved look. The bust has been lifted, and lowered, to suit the fashions of the time, and often comparatively heavy corsetry was necessary if you wanted to obtain the 'look' necessary to the clothes of the period. Thank goodness for the 'natural' look of today!

BODICE VARIATIONS

SHOULDER DART

a) Cut down the line **B–S**.

b) Close the side-bust dart, and the waist dart to produce the new dart **B–S–D**.

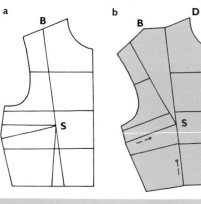

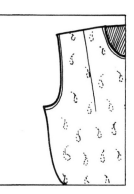

SHOULDER TUCKS

a) Extend the side-bust dart to point **H**. Cut down lines **A–S** and **B–H**.

b) Close the side-bust dart, and the waist dart. Stitch tucks down from the shoulder, or pleat the shoulder seam back to size.

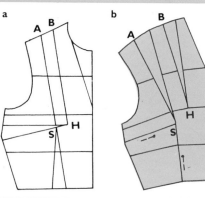

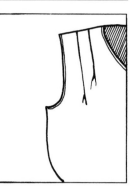

VEST INSERT

a) Cut down the line **B–S** and close out the side bust dart.

b) Draw line **S–C** and cut through to produce vest pattern. The bodice can hang loose ommiting the waist dart, or the waist can be taken back to size with gathers.

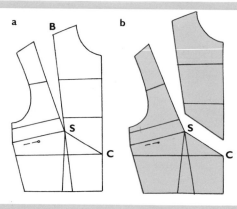

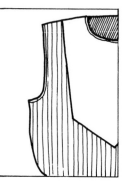

GATHERS IN CENTRE SEAM

a) Cut through the line **C–S**.

b) Close the side-bust dart, and also the waist dart. The centre front line is then gathered back to size.

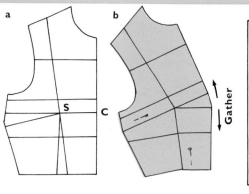

BODICE VARIATIONS

PLEATED SIDE SECTION

a) Cut out the waist and bust darts, and remove section **A–S–X–Y**. Divide this section into three parts.

b) Cut through these sections and spread **D**, **C** and **B**, leaving a 4cm gap where indicated.

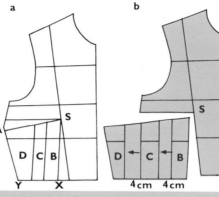

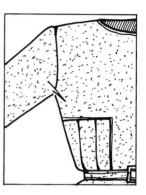

NECK DARTS

a) Move the side-bust dart into the armhole position. Draw the three lines, close the armhole dart, and spread the three sections as indicated. Stitch each section to form a dart, starting with the shortest at the top and increasing in length as they radiate towards the centre.

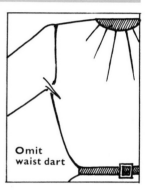

Radiating darts

Omit waist dart

GATHERED NECKLINE

a) Draw the new lines **A–S** and **B–H** and cut down the lines.

b) Close out the side-bust dart and the waist dart. Gather the neckline back to size.

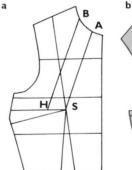

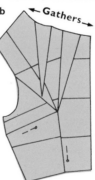

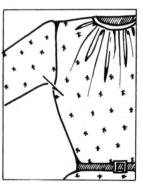

Gathers

HIGH COWL NECK

a) Raise the front neckline by 2.5cm to point **T**, and take the front shoulder line back by 2.5cm to point **A**. Draw the line (curved) **S–T**.

b) Cut through the line **S–T** and lift the line **A–T** until it is straight, at right angles to the centre front. Add a hem to the line **A–T**.

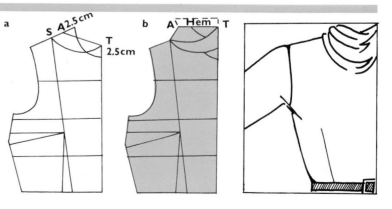

COWL NECKLINES

DOUBLE DRAPE

a) Mark point **A**, 10cm down from the centre front neck. Mark point **T**, 2.5cm in from the neck edge top. Join **A–T** and cut off. Draw curved lines **B–A** and **X–Y** as indicated.

b) Cut through these curved lines and spread them until line **T–A** is at right angles to a line drawn up from the waistline centre front. Move the waist dart into the side-bust dart.

c) The new pattern is best when cut on the direct cross grain of the fabric. A hem should be added to the top line **T–A**.

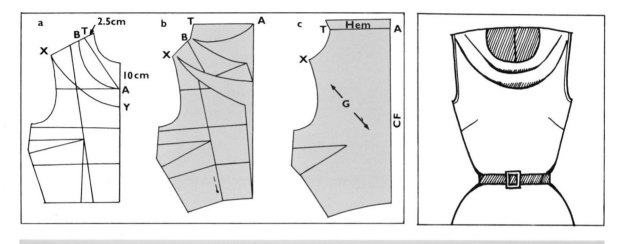

TRIPLE DRAPE

a) Mark point **A** 10cm down from the centre front neck. Mark point **T** 2.5cm in from the neck edge top. Joint **A–T** and cut off. Draw the curved lines **B–A**, **X–Y** and **Z–G** as indicated.

b) Cut these curved lines as indicated and spread the pieces until **A–T** is at right angles to a line drawn up from the waistline centre front. Move the waist dart into the side-bust dart.

c) The new pattern is best when cut on the direct cross grain of the fabric. A hem should be added to the top line **T–A**.

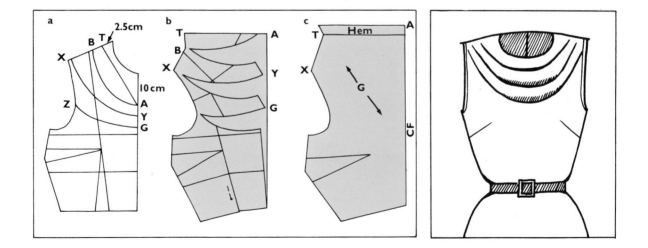

FRONT GATHERS

FRONT GATHERS

a) Draw the line **X–Y** approximately 8cm down from the top of the armhole. Draw lines **A–D** and **B–C**.

b) Cut down all three lines, close out the side-bust dart and the waist dart and spread the line

X–Y as indicated. Gather line **X–Y** back to fit original length.

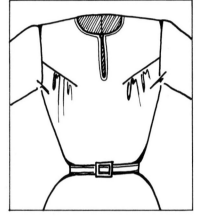

FRONT GATHERS

a) Draw the line **X–Y** and cut through to separate.

b) Close out the waist dart in the bottom section. Cut out the waist dart section left in the bodice and close the side dart.

This would give a gentle gather when **X–T** is gathered back to size.

c) Increased gathering can be obtained by cutting up the line **R–C** and spreading the side **X–A** as indicated.

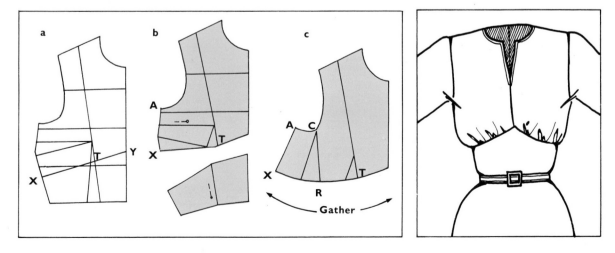

FRONT GATHERS

DRESS FRONT GATHERS

a) Drop the centre front neckline by 4cm and draw the new neckline. Draw the line **A–C–D** for the yoke effect and cut this section off the bodice.

b) Close the side-bust dart and cut through the pattern as indicated, cutting out the waist dart. Spread the pattern as indicated with about an 8cm gap at the waistline, depending on how much gather you require.

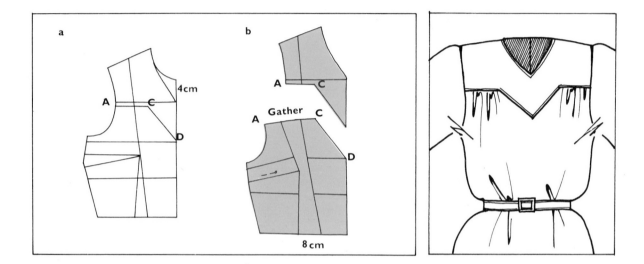

DRESS FRONT GATHERS

This is an attractive method of using a neck band, buttoned, to form a yoke.

a) Draw the curved line **A–C** and extend it by 5cm to draw the curved end **C–D**. Draw the three lines down from the yoke as illustrated.

b) Cut off the band **A–C**. Cut down the three drawn lines and close the side-bust dart and the waist dart, spread the line **A–C** evenly. A 10cm opening is allowed on the centre front.

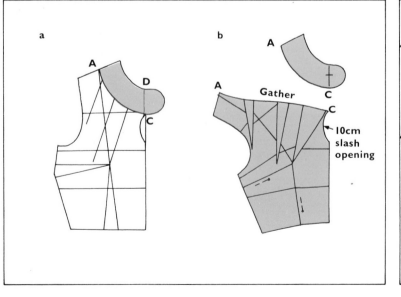

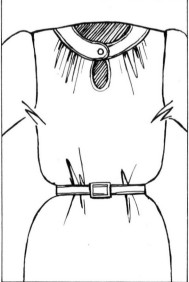

FRONT GATHERS

DRESS FRONT GATHERS

a) Drop the centre front neckline by 10cm, and draw in the new neckline. Draw line **A–C** (8cm) and **C–B** (leaving 4cm gap at the centre front). Cut piece **A–C–B** out to form the centre panel.

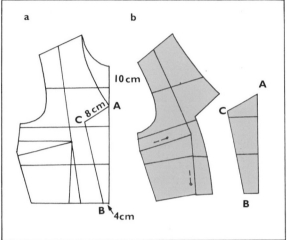

b) Close side-bust dart and waist dart.

c) Cut into the pattern and spread as indicated making each opening approximately 3cm. Gather this section up to fit the centre panel **A–C–B**.

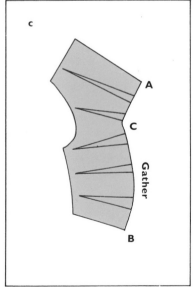

Bicorne in black velvet and panamalac from Reboux.
Blouse-like jacket in beige woollen material over crêpe blouse. Belted and buttoned with black. From Vionnet.

Patou hat of black bakou straw with pink grosgrain ribbon. Blouse of pink handkerchief linen with hemstitched band. Also Patou.

natural colour raffia hat lined with printed chiffon by Maria Guy. Blouse seen at the Ritz in the same printed chiffon worn with beige georgette suit.

Marie Alphonsine hat in black bakou with narrow leather belt around crown. Blouse from Lanvin in white crêpe de Chine with the new sleeve.

Marie Christiane hat in fancy straw in three colours with grosgrain band. Blouse from Jane Régny in white chiffon with smocking and crystal buttons.

COLLARS

Collars emerged as a status symbol. Heavily-jewelled gold necklaces, worn by both men and women, were separate from the main garment, and, in copying this idea, it became popular to use beads and embroidery around the neck of a garment to emulate the expensive jewellery. Gradually this embroidered area was made up as a separate piece, which could be interchanged on different garments, and this became the flat collar of today. Collar variations can be either close-fitting to the neck, or lying flat on the garment. They can be stitched into the garment, or can be made to take off which is useful for washing purposes. Collars can be incorporated into any neckline, and can often change the whole look of a garment, particularly if in a different colour or fabric. Matching a contrast introduced in another part of a good basic collar pattern, you can explore endless possibilities for use with your master pattern.

COLLARS

FLAT COLLAR

a) Place front and back shoulder seam together at the neck edge, overlap the armhole edge by 1.5cm. Lower front neck by 1.5cm. Draw new collar, to any depth required.

b) The new collar should be cut on the grain, as illustrated, and an under-collar will be required.

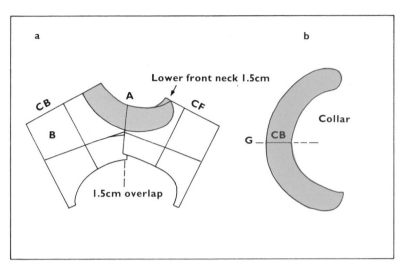

SAILOR-TYPE COLLAR

a) Place shoulder seams together as for the flat collar. Lower the front neck by 10cm. Draw new collar, noting that point **X** is a right angle.

b) The new collar can he hemmed at the edges and trimmed, or it can be cut with an under-collar.

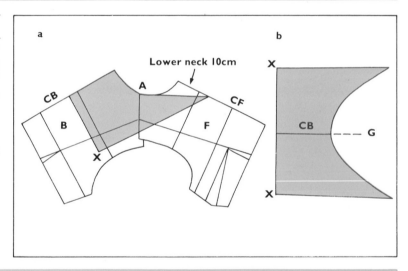

DOUBLE SAILOR COLLAR

a) Prepare shoulder seams as before. Lower front neck by 15cm. Draw new collars as illustrated.

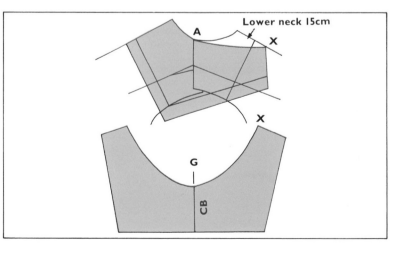

COLLARS

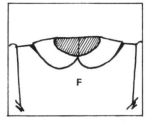

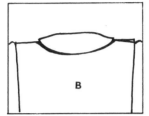

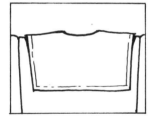

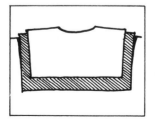

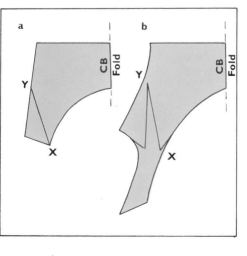

TO FORM TIES

a) Draw line **X–Y** and cut through.

b) Spread the pattern at point **X** and draw the new tie ends as required.

COLLARS

SEPARATE ROLL COLLARS

a) Draw neckline down 12cm from the centre front top. For the back draw **C–E** = 5cm. Draw **E–G** = **C–D** at right angles to the line **C–E**.

b) Draw **G–H** to centre shoulder. Make **E–J** = **G–H** plus 0.5cm.

c) Place the section **E–G–H–J** into position on the front shoulder line, noting that **H–G** on the back = **H–D** on the front. Draw the curved line **E–C**.

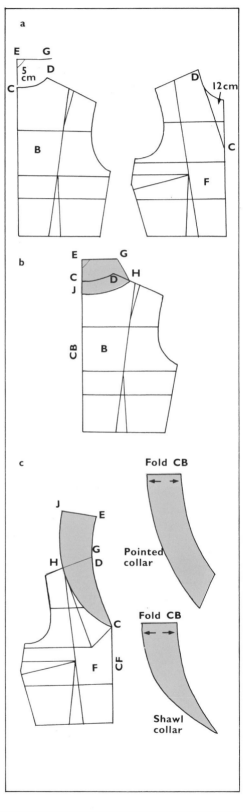

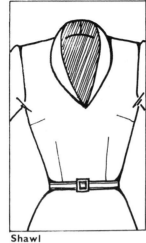

Shawl

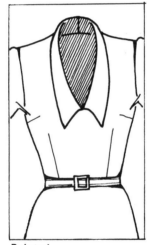

Pointed

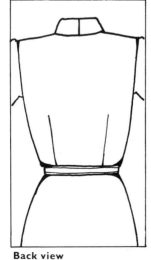

Back view

Imp. Lamoureux, r.S.te J.de Beauvais 12.

COLLARS

STAND COLLAR

This collar is most widely used. Meeting at the centre front of a garment, it fastens to a high neck. Alternatively it can be used as the collar part of a rever on a blouse or jacket.

a) Drop the front neck by 1.5cm to point **B**. Draw **B–C–D**, with **C–D** = half the back neck measurements.

b) Draw the curved line **C–B**.

c) Draw the 'mirrored' outer curve **C–B**.

d) Point **Z** is halfway on the outer curve **C–B**. Draw **Z–E** parallel to **B–D**. At right angles draw **E–X** to required collar width, passing through point **D**. Draw collar point **B–G**, point **G** being approximately 2.5cm from centre front. Join **X–G**.

e) Cut into the collar from the outer edge and spread the pattern, as illustrated to allow it to lie correctly on the shoulders.

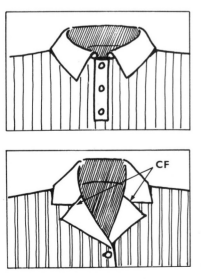

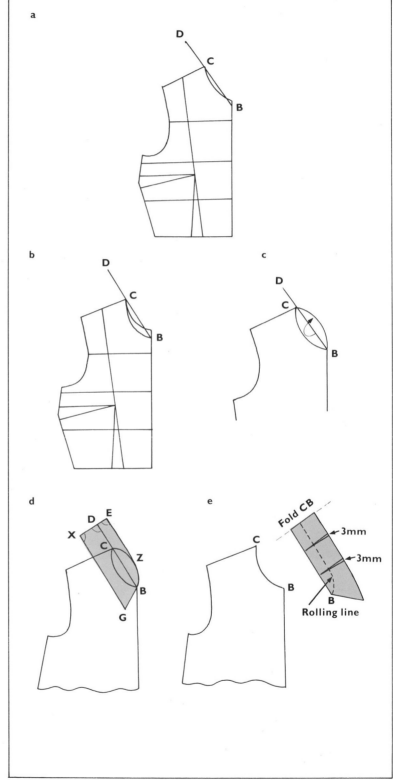

COLLARS

SHIRT COLLAR WITH SEPARATE

a) The shirt collar is used with a front fastening garment. An extension **B–G** has been added to form the wrap-over required. **B–G** = 4cm.

b) A–B = straight line
B–C = 2.5cm
C–D = **A–B** plus $\frac{1}{2}$ back neck measurement
D–E = 4cm

c) Join **E–B** with a gentle curve continuing to point **G**. **B–G** = amount of wrap-over from centre front. Draw curved line **G–C**.

d) Extend line **D–E** by 1cm to point **H**. Draw line **C–B–I** = 7cm. Draw line **H–I** curving from the point indicated.

e) The collar band and the outer collar together form the shirt collar.

f) To allow the outer collar to ease over the shoulder, cut the pattern as indicated and spread the sections, allowing a gap of 3mm at each point.

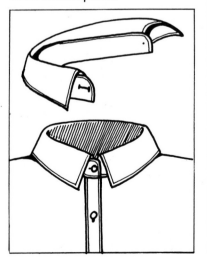

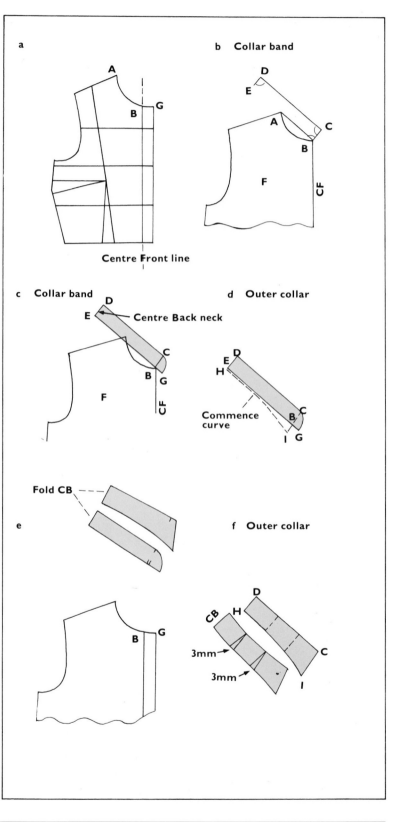

a

Centre Front line

b Collar band

c Collar band

Centre Back neck

d Outer collar

Commence curve

Fold CB

e

f Outer collar

3mm

3mm

EASY STRAIGHT-BAND COLLARS

CHINESE (MANDARIN) COLLAR

a) Make a rectangle which is 6cm deep, and ½ the size of the neckline lengthwise. Mark two 3mm darts.

b) Close the two darts and cut the curved front edge.

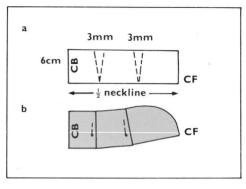

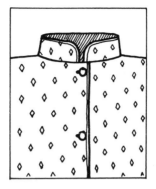

STRAIGHT COLLAR

This is the simplest collar used in garment making. The rectangle is made 6cm deep, and ½ the neckline in length. Extend the outer edge by 2.5cm and draw the line to the centre front point.

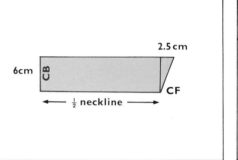

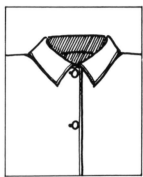

SMALL STAND COLLAR

Used with the rever on page 89. To make the collar stand higher, and sit closer to the neck, add 2cm to the **CB** edge and join this point **X** to the point **CF**. Extend the outer edge by 1cm and draw the line to the **CF**.

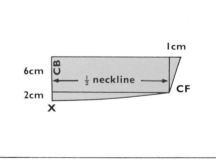

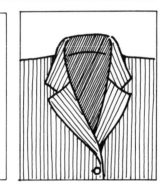

WIDER BAND COLLAR

a) Make the rectangle 6cm deep and half the neckline in length. Mark dotted lines **X** and **Y**.

b) Cut down lines **X** and **Y** and spread the collar outer edge. Extend the **CB** by 3cm at the neck edge, and draw the collar points as illustrated.

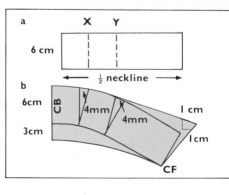

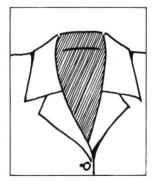

EASY STRAIGHT-BAND COLLARS

COLLARLESS JACKET

a) Decide how low you want the rever to open, and mark this point **R**. Decide width of rever and mark point **X**. Join **P** to **R**, **P** to **X** and **X** to **R**.

b) Cut piece **P–C–R** away from the bodice front, and place the rever **P–X–R** into position as illustrated.

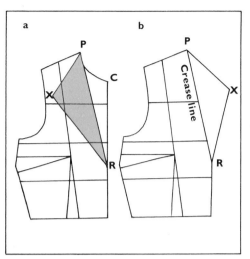

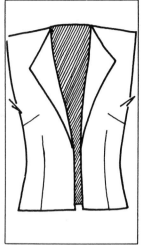

OPEN REVERS

Allow 3cm wrap to centre front edge.
This is widely used for blouses and jackets. The normal neckline is folded back to any chosen level. The small stand collar from p. **88** is stitched to the centre front point **C** to complete the rever.

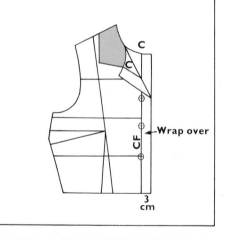

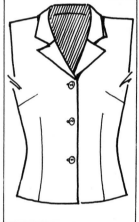

SHAPED REVERS

Allow 3cm wrap to centre front edge.
a) Draw the new rever **N–X–R**.

b) Add the collar from page 88, stitched to centre front **C**.

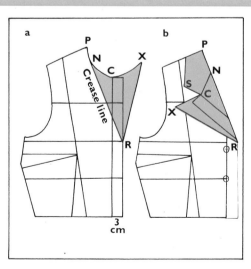

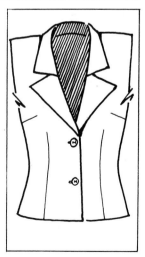

ROLL COLLARS

HIGH ROLL COLLAR

Allow 3cm wrap to centre front edge.

a) The roll collar is cut in one with the front of the garment. Select point **N** and draw line **N–P** extended to **X**. Place the two neck edges **P** together, and place the centre back neck-edge on point **X**. Draw the roll collar **X–CB–N**.

b) The new pattern indicated the crease line **P–N**.

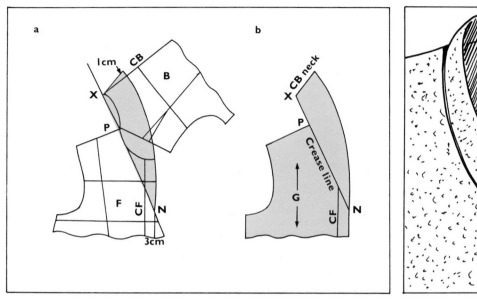

STORM COLLAR

Allow 3cm wrap to centre front edge.

a) Select point **N** and draw **N–P** continuing to point **Z**. Place the shoulder points together at **P** and place point **X** approximately 4cm over the line **P–Z**. Draw new collar **X–R–S–N**.

b) The new pattern indicated the crease line **P–N**.

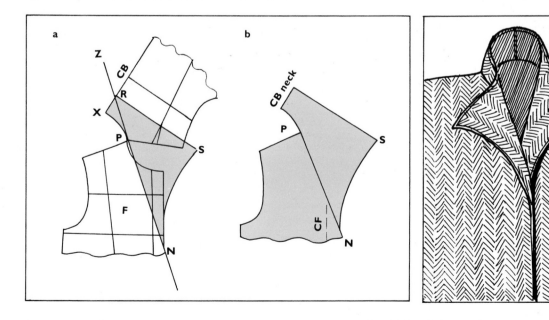

CUFFS

Cuffs have always been used as a method of decoration at the bottom of sleeves. Often made separately from the main garment they could be made of elaborate or delicate fabric, which enabled them to be removed for washing purposes. Cuffs could also be an extension of the sleeve length, simply turned up to wrist length.

BLOUSE OR SHIRT CUFF

a) Fabric should be cut from folded edge, and is the length of the wrist size plus 4cm extensions at each end.

b) With the ends stitched, as illustrated, and turned to the right side of fabric, the sleeve can be gathered to fit the edge **F–B**. **Note:** The sleeve opening should always be on the back line.

ADDED CUFF

a) Decide the depth of cuff required and mark this on your sleeve pattern. **A–B–C–D**.

b) This type of cuff is usually cut with the fold at line **A–B**. Alternatively, you can cut two pieces **A–B–C–D** which would allow for either lining or contrast fabric to be used.

LONG CUFF

a) Create new top sleeve to any chosen length.

b) Cut the bottom sleeve into four sections, **A**, **B**, **C** and **D**. Overlap the sections so that **X–Y** = wrist measurement and **R–S** = middle arm measurement. Place section **A** next to section **D**.

CUFFS

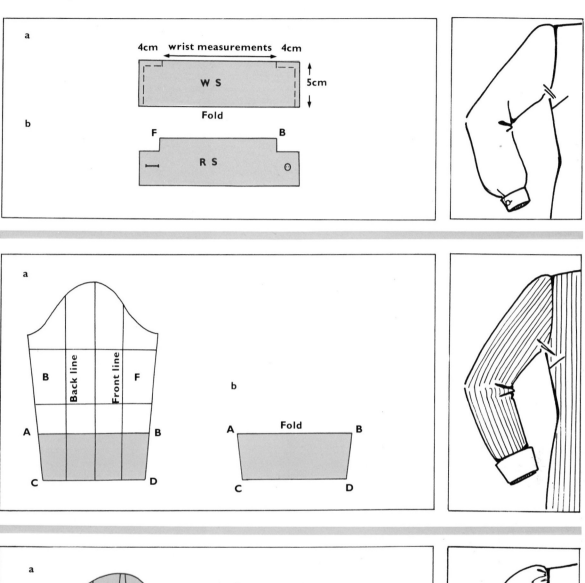

a

4cm   wrist measurements   4cm

W S

5cm

Fold

b

F   B

R S

a

B   Back line   Front line   F

A   B

C   D

b

A   Fold   B

C   D

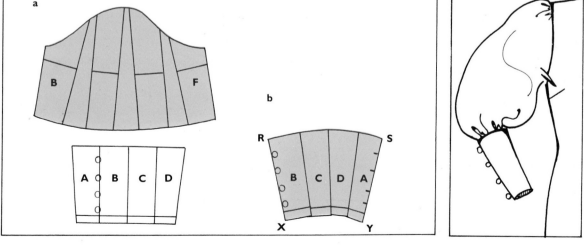

a

B   F

A   B   C   D

b

R   S

B   C   D   A

X   Y

CUFFS

TRIMMED CUFFS

Lace trimming can be inserted between the two layers of fabric which are forming the cuff.
a) Measure the distance around the edge **A–D** and use twice this length of lace to form the trim. Stitch gathered lace into place on to one cuff piece, then bring remaining piece over and stitch again.

b) Turn cuff to right side.

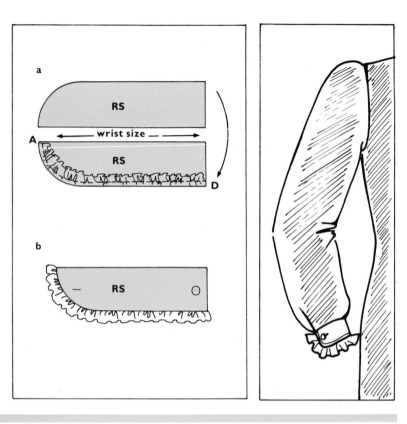

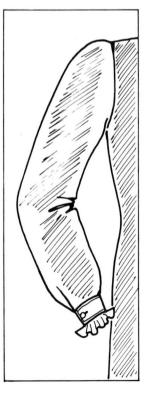

2a) Measure **A–D** and take twice this length of lace. Gather the lace and stitch to bottom edge. Bring remaining piece over and stitch again.

b) Turn cuff to right side.

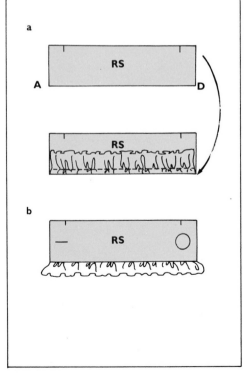

CUFFS

WRAP-OVER FRONTS

The development from edge to edge garments, which were often laced together, into the general use of button and buttonhole to fasten a garment, gave further scope to clothes designers. Fastening a garment with buttons and buttonholes became a focal point for decoration, and just as cutting lines and darts can be moved, so could the fastening position. The simple wrap-over, on page 98, is still the most widely used in blouse and shirt making and this method also forms the basis for many jackets and suits. Centre front fastening is most common, but double-breasted fastening, shoulder fastening and fastening down one side only are but a few of the many variations used in the fashion industry.

WRAP-OVER FRONTS

SIMPLE WRAP

Cut the front with a 3cm extension over the **CF** line.

Note: Buttonholes are best placed $\frac{1}{3}$ over the **CF** line and $\frac{2}{3}$ into the bodice. Cut facing as illustrated.

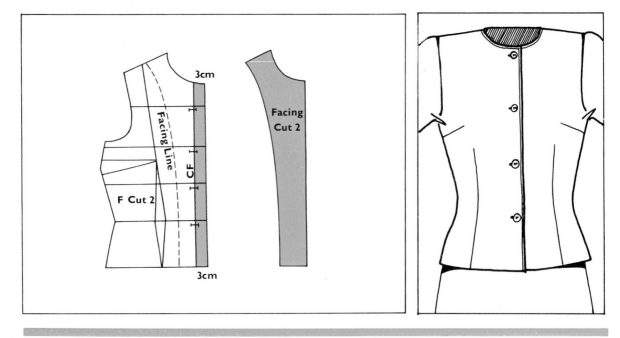

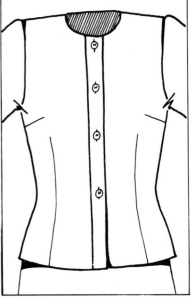

STRAP FRONT BAND

a) Cut a band 8cm wide, and as long as the centre front.

b) Fold band in half and stitch to centre front edge.

c) Press band over, as illustrated.

Note: Vertical buttonholes in the band.

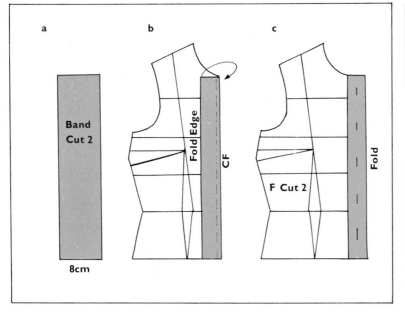

WRAP-OVER FRONTS

DOUBLE-BREASTED WRAP

Extend the **C** front by 8cm.
Mark buttonholes equidistant from centre front line.
Cut facings as illustrated.

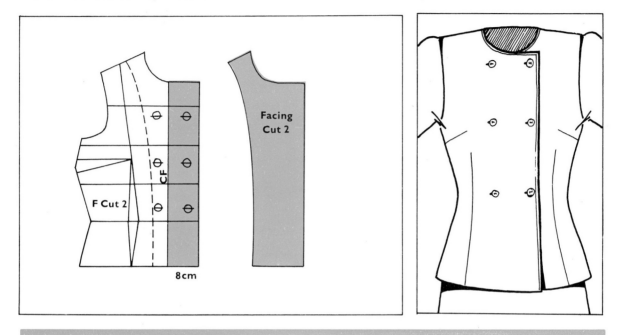

SIDE WRAP

a) Cut through the pattern from point **A** through the middle of the dart to point **D**.

b) Allow a 3cm wrap from points **A–D** out to points **X–Y**.

Facings. Cut as for extension on right front and left front.

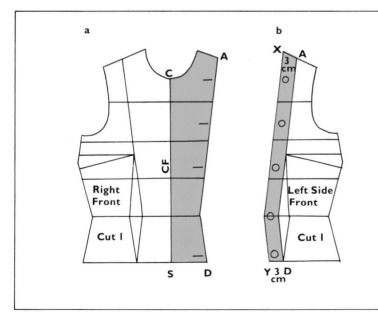

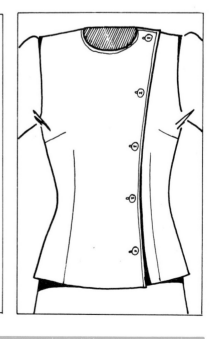

CAPES

From the earliest days of the Roman *toga*, the cape effect can be traced throughout the history of costume and in all civilizations. The cape could be worn as an outer-garment worn over narrow, or wide gowns. It was worn through the centuries by the feudal lord of the manor and his soldiers. The rough sacking cloaks of the peasant were in complete contrast to the elaborate cloaks worn by the rulers, and by the hierarchy of religious orders. Often worn as a regal, ceremonial garment, the cape has come forward into today's world of fashion, and appears regularly in either long, short or medium length as fashions change.

CAPES

LOOSE CAPE

Place the front and back bodices together at the shoulder seam. Decide the length of cape required and mark this down the centre front **T–A**. Mark the same length down the centre back **H–D** and also along the shoulder line **N–X**. Connect up the points **D–X–A** as illustrated. Mark point **S** to be 6cm out from point **X** on the shoulder line. Draw the edge of the cape **D–S–A**.

Note: 6cm at **S–X** allows cape to rise over the shoulder and drop to an even length around the bottom.

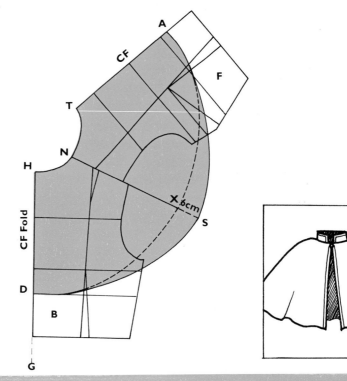

SHAPED CAPE

Cut through the line **N–S** and overlap the bottom edge of the cape to reduce the fullness. This produces the dart **N–X–N** which finishes at the shoulder edge.

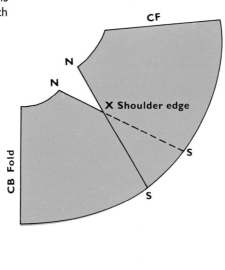

CAPES

FULL-LENGTH FLARED CAPE

Move the front side-bust dart into the shoulder position. Place shoulders together at point **N**, making the distance **X–Y** equal a quarter of the bust measure-ment. Select length required, and measure down the centre front and centre back to this measurement to point **S**. The line **N–T** bisects line **X–Y** and is equal in length to **CB**, and **CF** plus 5cm to allow for shoulder lift.

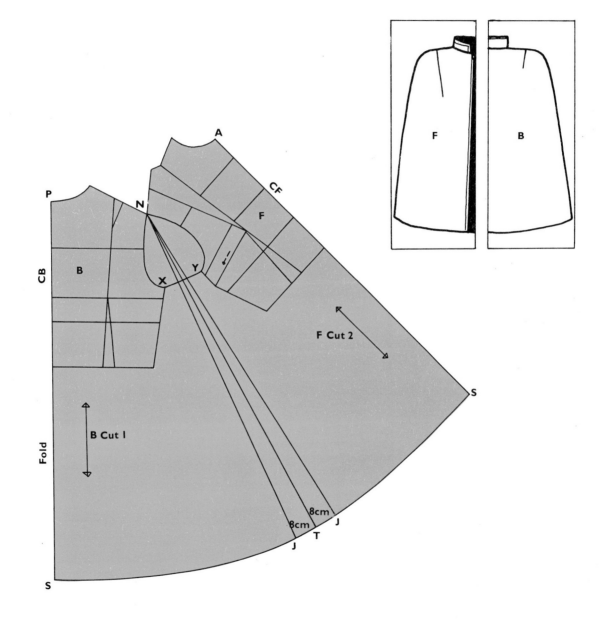

CAPES

CAPE WITH SIDE PANELS AND GATHERED SHOULDERS

a) Move front side-bust dart into the shoulder position. Place shoulder edges together as illustrated. **X–Y** = quarter of bust measurement. Draw curved side panels **R–S–T**, noting that the curve takes in one side of the back shoulder dart, and one side of the front shoulder dart.

b) For the new pattern: cut the three sections of the patterns, and separate them, mark the positions where they will re-join when stitched. On the centre panel cut down from **S–P** and spread the pattern at point **S**. This gives the gathers for the shoulders whilst, at the same time, narrowing the edge. Cut to any chosen length. An opening for the hands could be positioned on the front seam.

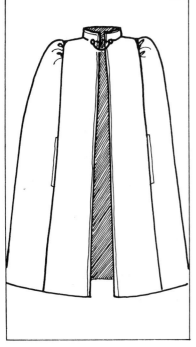

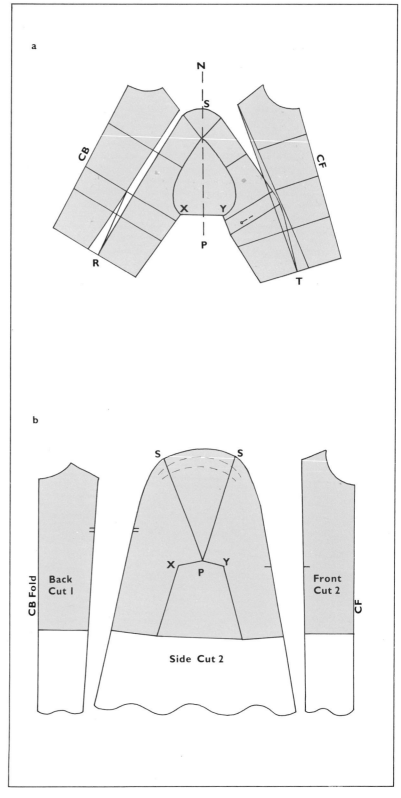

CAPES

COLLARS AND A SIMPLE HOOD

Any collar can be attached to the cape pattern in exactly the same way as to a blouse or jacket.

a) Prepare a rectangle of paper 30cm × 40cm.

b) Draw hood pattern as illustrated. **N** = centre back neck. Line **N–CF** = half the neckline measurement, and can be eased to fit.

c) Stitch line **R–N**, then fold the hood to stitch the top opening.

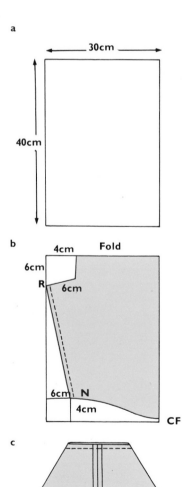

SKIRTS

The changing face of female fashion can usually be dated by the outline of the skirt silhouette. Right until the end of the nineteenth century the shape of the skirts were controlled by frames, hoops, padding, and underskirts, and it was not until after the First World War, that the natural shape of the female body became the basis for the fashion of the day. This was particularly reflected in the skirt, which became fashionable as a separate item, and still forms the basis for many of the coordinated outfits designed today.

SKIRTS

THE BASIC SKIRT

a) The part below the waist on the block pattern is the starting base for all skirts. Because of the difficulties often encountered in placing the opening in the curved side-hip seam, a centre-back opening should be considered when making up the majority of skirts.

b) The basic skirt pattern will need to fit closely at the waist, to support the skirt. To obtain a closer fit, the side seams can be shaped to the required size, as illustrated.

c) The angle of the front waist dart can also be changed to give a smoother fit to the front skirt. Line **A–B** will be lowered by approximately 0.5cm when this is done.

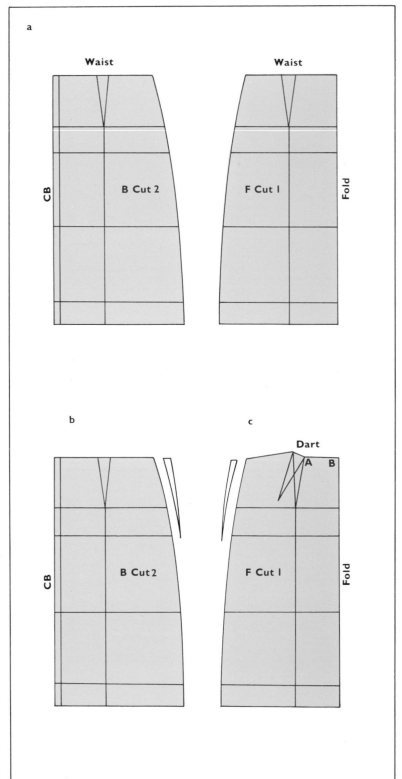

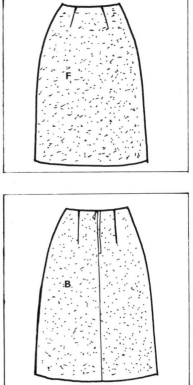

SKIRTS

INVERTED FRONT PLEAT

Place **CF** of the skirt 12cm away from the folded edge of the fabric. Stitch down the centre front to point **X**, and press pleat as illustrated.

Note: The basic back pattern can be used with this front.

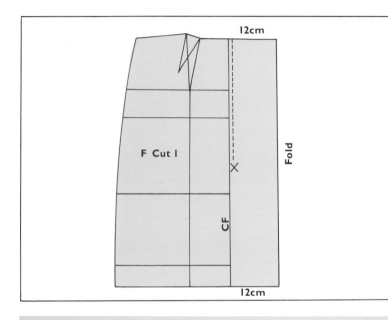

BACK INVERTED PLEAT

Proceed as for the front, placing **CB** approximately 12cm from fold of fabric. A side opening will be necessary.

Note: The basic front pattern can be used with this back.

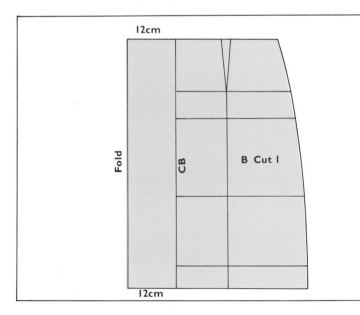

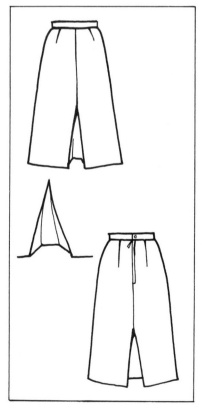

SKIRTS

4-GORE FLARED SKIRT

Cut up the lines **X–Y** and **A–D** and close out the waist darts. Extend a line from the second hip on the side seams to allow added flare.

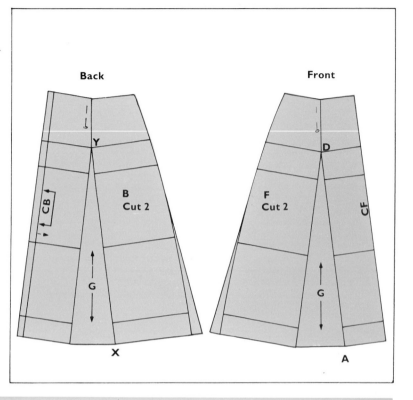

6-GORE SKIRT

Cut up the lines **X–Y** and **A–D**, as for the 4-gore skirt, except that you cut out completely the waist darts. Add flare to all seams except the **CB** and cut the centre front to the fold of the fabric.

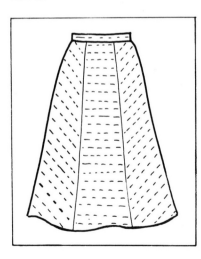

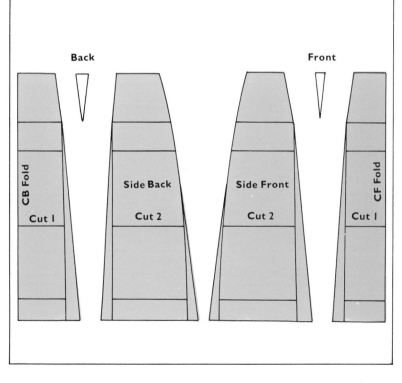

SKIRTS

SIDE PANELS CUT AS ONE

As for the 6-gore skirt cut up the lines **X–Y** and **A–D**, and completely cut out the waist darts.

Place the side seams together down to the 2nd hip line, which will allow this area to now be cut as one piece, doing away with the side seams, and giving a slight flare to the side panels. Keep the **CF** and **CB** on the straight grain but add a flare to the remaining seam edge as illustrated.

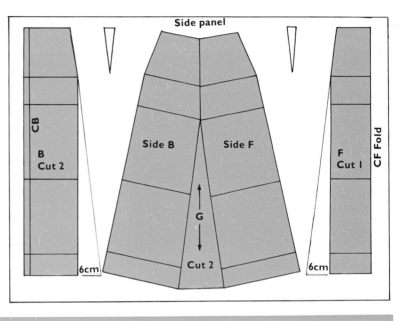

FRONT PANEL SKIRT (WITH POCKET)

Used with basic Back Pattern
Cut through the pattern **X–R**, noting that this is to the side of the dart. Divide the centre section into three parts and spread, as illustrated. Ignore the waist darts, which become part of the centre panel gathers. Cut four pocket pieces to depth **X–Y**, if required.

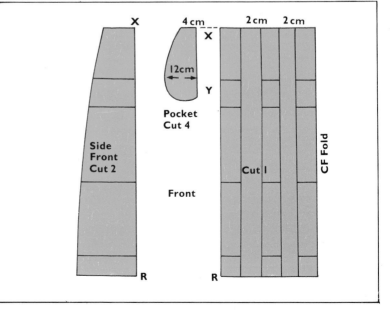

SKIRTS

POSITIONING PLEATS AND DARTS

a) The position of darts **A**, **B**, **C** on the front and back pattern, together with the line **C–D** are fixed by the bust position on the Basic Block. When using the skirt as a separate pattern, alternatives can be used.

b) The dart **A–B–C** front and back can be divided into two smaller darts, which give a smoother fit when stitched.

c) When pleats are inserted in the skirt they can be placed in any position by moving the dart **A–B–C** and the line **C–D** into a different position.

Ideally point **D** is best positioned halfway between **X–Y** on the skirt hem.

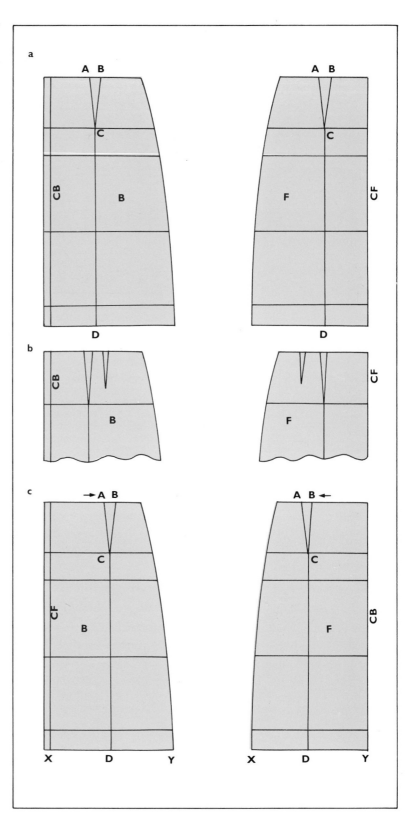

SKIRTS

INSET INVERTED PLEAT FRONT AND BACK WITH SIDE OPENING

Front: Having selected the position for the pleat at point **D** cut through the pattern and remove the dart. Spread the pattern, making **A–B** = 24cm to form the pleat.

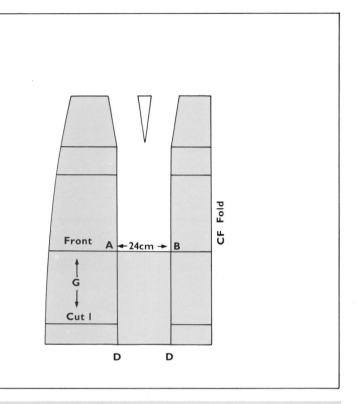

ALTERNATIVE

The section **A–B–C–D** can be cut as separate piece, and can be very effectively used in contrast fabric. This method can be applied to either the front or back of the skirt. The section **A–B–C–D** can be replaced with a godet, cut as a quarter circle **D–AB–D**.

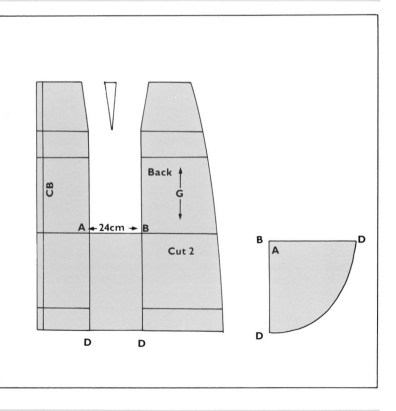

SKIRTS

CIRCULAR SKIRT USING BASIC BLOCK

Using the basic front skirt block cut the pattern into three sections, **A**, **B** and **C**, and remove the waist dart. Place the waist edges together and draw a smooth quarter circle line **X–R**. Measure the length **R–S** and **X–Y**.

Note: Angles **S** and **Y** are right-angles. Draw the hem line **S–Y**, measuring from the quarter circle **X–R** at regular intervals to keep a level hem.

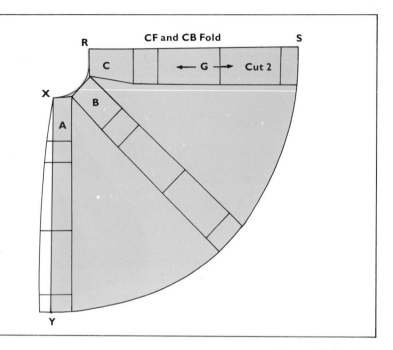

MATHEMATICAL METHOD

Waist circumference = $C = 2\pi r$ (or wrist, or neckline measurement)

$$C = 2 \times \frac{22}{7} \times R \quad (R = \text{radius})$$

$$7C = 44R$$

$$R = \frac{7C}{44} \text{ i.e. } \frac{7 \times \text{Waistsize}}{44}$$

Note: Above method can also be used to calculate frills for neck and wrist.

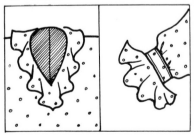

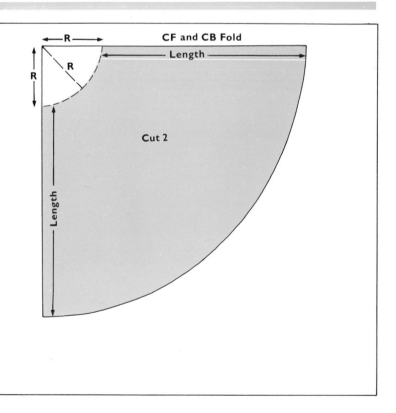

SKIRTS

SKIRTS

YOKED SKIRT WITH FRONT PLEATS

a) Take the front and back basic skirt block and cut through them on the second hip-line.

b) Close out the waist darts on both the front and back yokes. Cut the side section of the front skirt into three parts and spread as illustrated to form pleats.

a   Back   Front

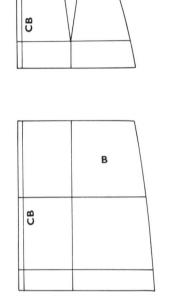

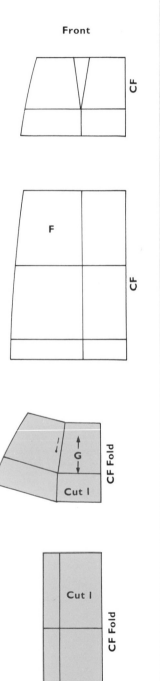

b

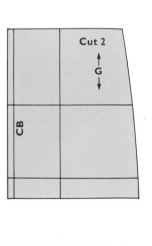

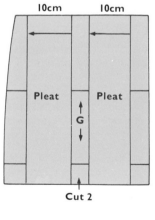

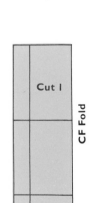

SKIRTS

FLARED WRAP-ROUND SKIRT

Place front and back pattern pieces together, as illustrated.
Note: The waist darts that are closed out, and the one remaining but omitted.
Also note: The grain line for cutting.
A = Side seams overlapping
D = Centre back
C = Centre front.

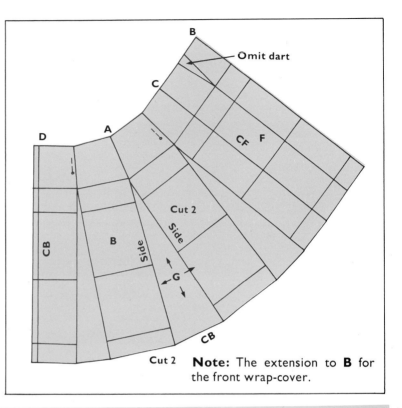

Note: The extension to **B** for the front wrap-cover.

PEG-TOP SKIRT

a) Instead of using the waist dart, draw line **X–Y** = to waist dart, and cut this away. Draw lines **A–B** and **C–D**.

b) Cut down lines **A–B** and **C–D**, and spread pattern at the waist-line, as required.

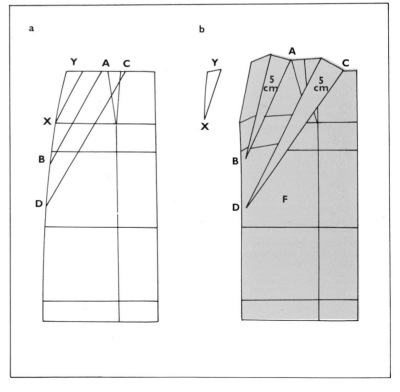

SKIRTS AND TROUSERS

WAISTBAND METHODS

ELASTICATED

a) Insert the elastic into the waistband, using a safety pin, and taking care not to twist it inside the casing.

b) Pull the elastic through the hem casing, overlap the ends, and stitch them securely.

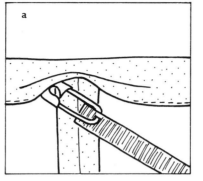

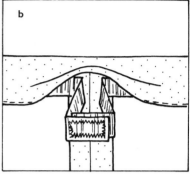

CURVED PETERSHAM

a) Stitch the inside curve of petersham to the right side of the waistline. Allow 2cm of petersham to overlap at each end.

b) Turn petersham over to the inside. Attach hooks, and catch the petersham to the darts and side seams.

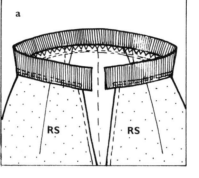

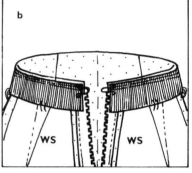

ADDED WAISTBAND

Using Vilene 'Fold-a-band' interfacing.

a) Waist size + 5cm. Iron on interfacing.

b) Stitch one edge of waistband to the waistline, as indicated.

c) Fold the waistband, and stitch the edges for overlap fastening.

d) Turn band to the right side, then stitch remaining edge on wrong side of garment.

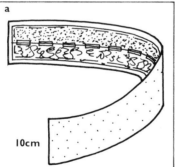

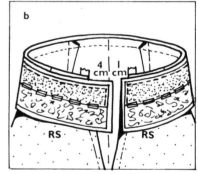

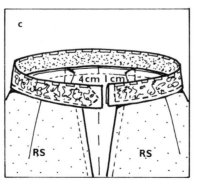

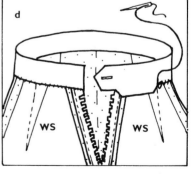

TROUSERS

Trousers, long worn as pyjamas, and much earlier as bloomers have become increasingly popular in female fashion. Bicycling brought in the divided skirt, and cruising and beach wear soon became popular day-wear. The Second World War saw women working along side the men, and, indeed, wearing trousers both as uniform, and for relaxation. The recent increase in leisure and sporting activities has increased the use of trousers for women, and the 'jean-scene' has completely unisexed this type of outfit. The relationship of the skirt to trousers (or 'pants') can be clearly seen in the block pattern section of the book, where the trouser pattern is taken directly from the skirt pattern.

121

TROUSERS

THE SIMPLEST TROUSER WITHOUT SIDE SEAMS

The front and back pattern are placed with the side seams touching. The **CB** waistline is raised by 2cm to point **X**, dropping to point **Y** at the front. A top hem of 3cm is added to allow for elastic, or a tie, to be inserted.

Note: The darts are not used.

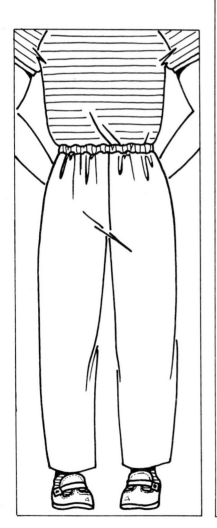

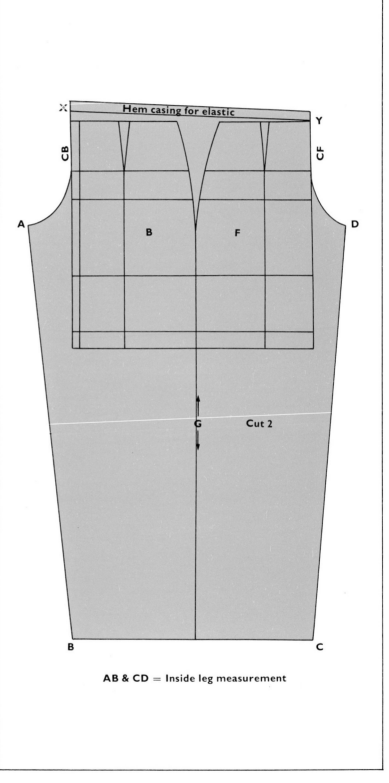

AB & CD = Inside leg measurement

TROUSERS

THE ALTERNATIVES

The successful fit of trousers depends upon three essential fitting points:

a) The crutch **A–C–D–B** must be the correct length for your body.

b) The waistline must be correctly fitted.

c) The hip fitting should be correct at the 2nd hip-line.

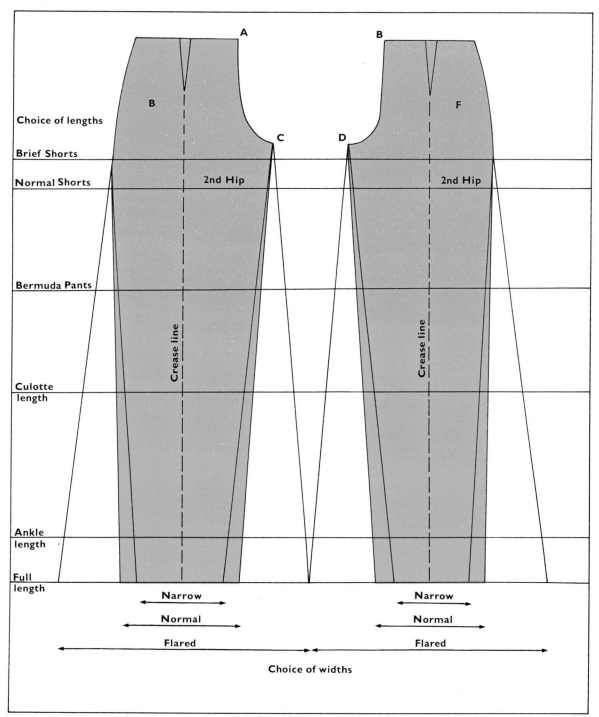

DIVIDED SKIRT

THE DIVIDED SKIRT

Note: The pleat is added to the **CF** and **CB** lines on the pattern. Both the front and back pattern are cut through on these lines, and a 10cm allowance is let in to form the pleat. A slight flare should be added to the side seams from the 2nd hip-line.

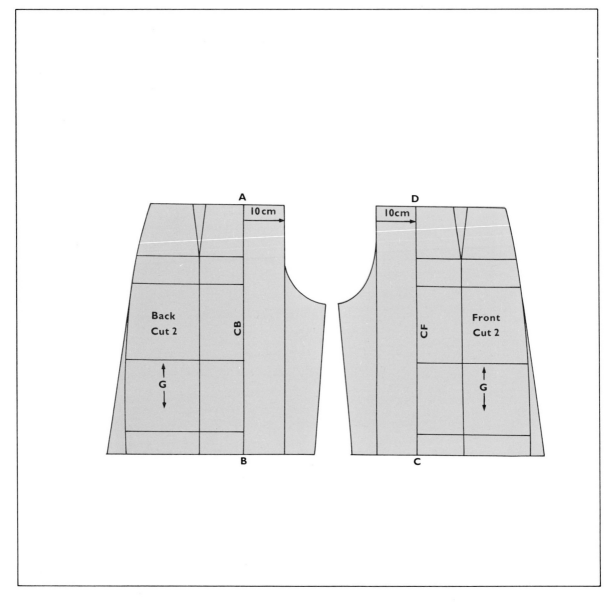

SHORTS

SHORTS

To ensure that the shorts fit closely to the top of the leg, the side seam and the crutch seam should be shaped, as illustrated.

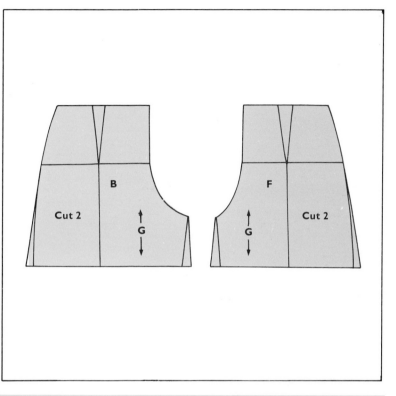

FRONT PLEATED SHORTS

a) Cut the yoke off the front pattern and close out the waist dart.

b) Divide the **F** bottom section into three and spread, as illustrated, to produce the pleats. Add a slight flare to both the front and back side seams.

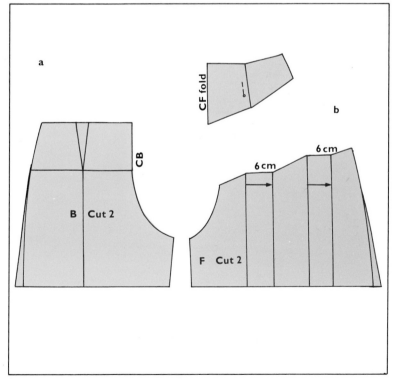

Last = Minute Sketches from Cannes

Maria Guy
Béret and scarf in navy taffeta combined with white-dotted taffeta

Vionnet

Coat in grey and blue tweed, blue leather belt. Blue and grey Agnès turban.

Vionnet

Schiaparelli

Madame Agnès wears this suit. Red toile de laine jacket, blue skirt and blue tie. Blue and red jersey turban

Hand-woven tweed black on pink with a white line. Agnès turban of black lacy hemp with satin bow.

Jean Dunand has made for Madame Agnès this set of heavy silver jewellery.

Suit of navy blue man's material, with a pale grey pin stripe. New sailor hat in navy straw, blue satin across the forehead.

Louise boulanger

CREATING
FASHION TODAY

The speed of fashion change has gathered momentum dramatically since the early part of the twentieth century. Fast communication of ideas would change the fashions all over the world, within days of it being presented to the press. The eagerly-awaited Paris shows directed the look for the coming season. Designer's names came into prominence and some, such as Chanel, will remain forever identified with a certain 'look'. Although Paris dominated the fashion scene for many years, by the 1950's the emphasis had begun to change to other centres. London, Rome, Milan, Tokyo and America were all producing exciting young designers, with a fresh outlook, particularly in the growing man-made fabric industry, which, together with the knitted fabrics available in all weights and textures gave a greater freedom to experiment. The mass production of ready-to-wear garments and the affluent society able to buy them constantly demanded more and more dramatic changes, so that the customer would be eager to buy the latest ideas. The manufacturers needed only a sketch from the designs of a master 'couture' fashion house to send their patternmakers scurrying to their studios to copy the ideas and adapt them for the mass market. If you have worked through this book and tried out the ideas _ if only in small scale _ you will have discovered how patterns are created, and you should be able to 'read' a sketch or photograph as a competent patternmaker. Looking into the history of costume will make you quickly realise that, today, there is seldom anything completely new in fashion. A re-mix of the pattern pieces, together with a change of fabric and accessories, can produce today's fashion. To do it for yourself you need only a Basic Master Pattern that fits, and the knowledge of how to make it work.

HORIZONTAL PATTERN

THE HORIZONTAL PATTERN

To practise designing clothes you would be well advised to make a copy of your Basic Master Pattern in stiff card, and divide it into the sections **A**, **B**, **C**, **D**, **E**, **F** so that you can experiment with different combinations of pieces.

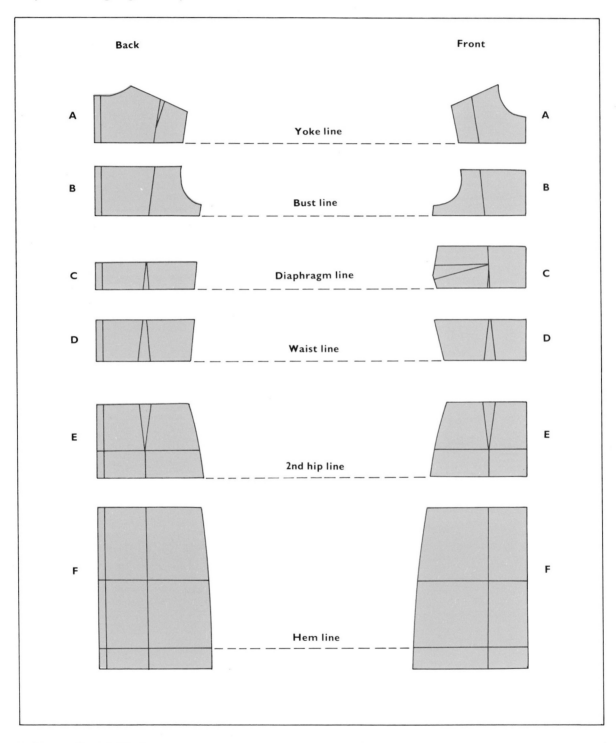

Back   Front

A — Yoke line — A

B — Bust line — B

C — Diaphragm line — C

D — Waist line — D

E — 2nd hip line — E

F — Hem line — F

VERTICAL PATTERN

THE VERTICAL PATTERN

Many designs are developed by cutting the pattern vertically into the sections **1**, **2**, **3**, **4**, **5** on the front, and **1**, **2** and **3** on the back. This you should also do in stiff card so that you can experiment and combine different sections to create new lines.

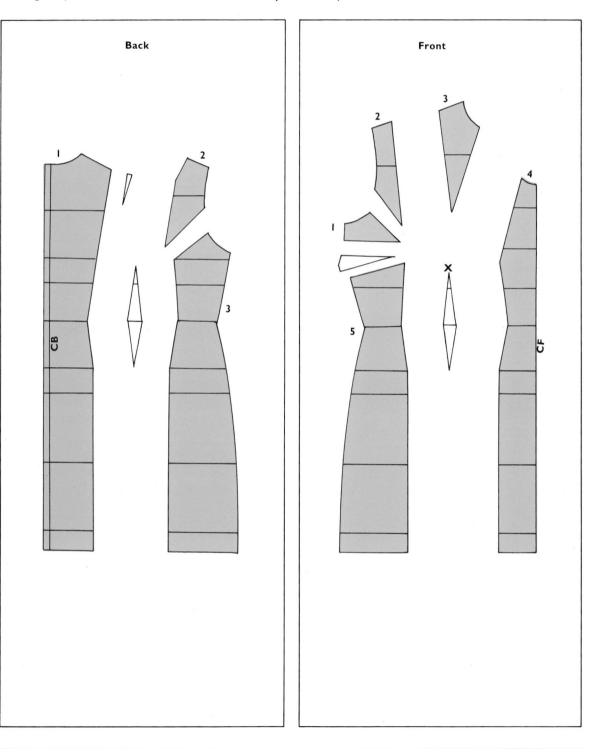

Back

Front

EARLY PATTERN INSTRUCTIONS

If you study some of the early printed pattern instructions you must remember that they were going to be followed by the 'little dressmaker round the corner' who understood what to do by just looking at the diagram. Once the dressmaker had made a garment to fit her client she kept the pattern, and used it as the basis for any other style that her customer might order, taking ideas from the fashionable catalogues of the day.

Having worked through this book you will have discovered, as I did, that making patterns is not a mysterious specialist subject, it was just that, with the introduction of commercial paper patterns, we lost a skill. Commercial patterns, in standard sizes, appeared to be a much easier option to the home dressmaker who wanted to make her own clothes and so the necessity to pass on the old skills and to teach the working-pattern was gradually phased out. But, the apparent ease of using commercial patterns was to prove the stumbling block if not the deterrent to many a home dressmaker. The simple reason being, that we do not have standard size people.

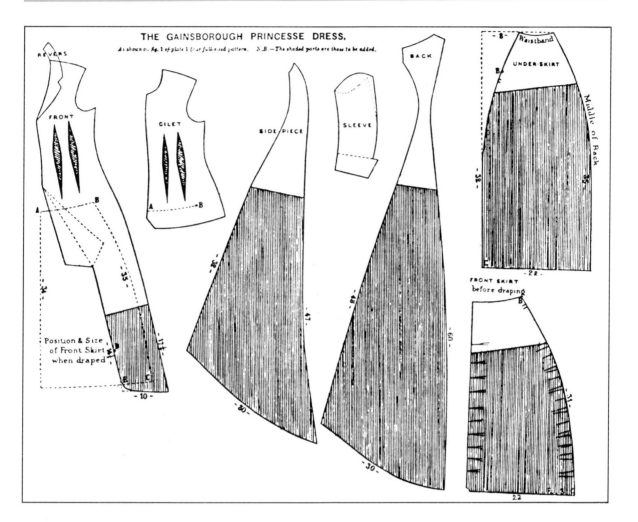

THE GAINSBOROUGH PRINCESSE DRESS.

As shown on fig. 1 of plate 1 (our full-sized pattern). N.B.—The shaded parts are those to be added.

1 Detail from fashion plate, diagram and instructions for the Gainsborough Princesse Dress, from *Paris Ladies Magazine of Fashion.* January 1879.

2 Diagram of the New Skirt from *Myra's Journal of Dress and Fashion.* 1 March 1878:

'The half of the new skirt is shown on our diagram: it consists of three pieces, the front; which has a small gore to shape it exactly to the figure; the side and back, which are cut in one; and the top the back width on which the train pleats are fastened.'

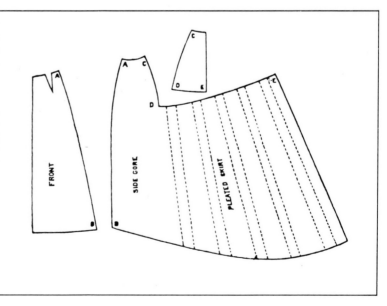

Front and back view and diagram of the cut-out pattern of the 'Druscovitch Corsage', from Myra's Journal of Dress and Fashion, 1 August 1884.

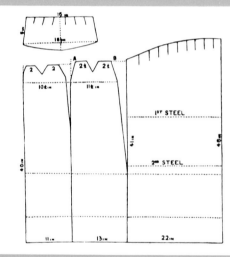

Diagram of foundation skirt and cushion from Dressmaking Lessons Part II by 'Myra', 1888.

A new skirt for 27-inch material, from *Le Moniteur de la Mode, The Lady's Magazine*. 1 Sept 1893.
'Drill, which has been so much in demand for country toilettes, is only 27" wide. As most fabrics are double width, it necessitated a new shape of skirt. It is the very thing for velveteen. The drill skirt and dark overblouse has been adopted generally for seaside tennis, the smooth sandy beach replacing the velvet lawn. The lower edge of the skirt measures 3¾ yards, quite enough now that the knell of the full "Bell" skirt is rung.'

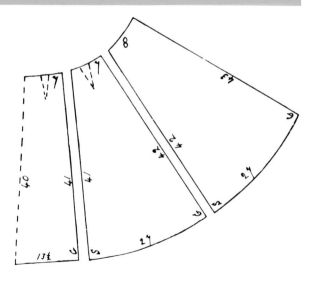

EARLY PATTERN INSTRUCTIONS

Front view and diagram of a draped bodice trimmed with velvet from Le Moniteur de la Mode. The Lady's Magazine, 1 April 1982:

'The bodice is made up on a lining cut like Figs. 1, 2, 3 and 4 of the diagram. . . The fastening is on one side and the centre, between the slanting lines, is covered with velvet, which may be pleated or laid on flat, but which must be without a seam. The draped fronts are cut like No 5, with fine pleats at the shoulder and again at the waist; the front edge is the selvedge way of the material. . . The back, No 6, is also arranged in pleats at the top leaving a small V-shaped opening to be covered in velvet. . . This makes a very pretty and simple morning gown for young ladies and looks well in grey and black, fawn and black and in any of the plain rather light coloured woollens that are always in the spring.'

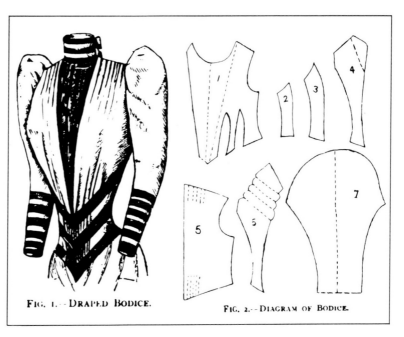

FIG. 1.—DRAPED BODICE.

FIG. 2.—DIAGRAM OF BODICE.

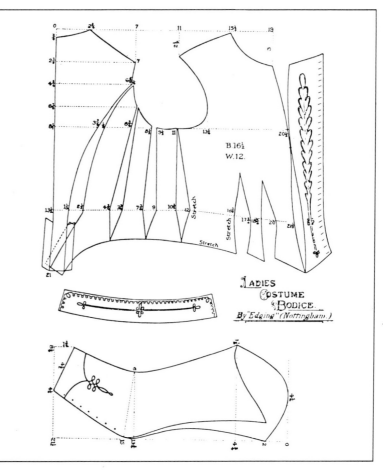

Diagram of a ladies' costume, bodice and sleeve from *Ladies Garment Cutting* by T H Holding, 1890.

PATTERN FOR FITTED BODICE

BASIC BODICE WITH OR WITHOUT STRAPS

a) The basic bodice gives the opportunity of deciding the cutting lines, which can be used to fit in with any requirements. At the same time it gives the length of any shoulder straps required. The fluted peplum used in the right-hand dress can be created, as illustrated, in four pieces. **Note:** The darts in the skirt have been removed.

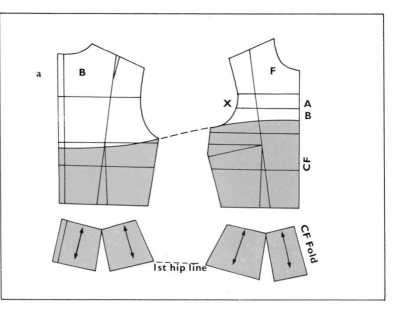

b) The Back Bodice. Used for both styles. Cut the bodice, as indicated, close waist dart and overlap 2cm at the top edge to give tighter fit.

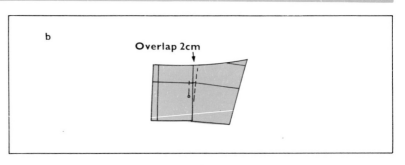

c) Front Bodice (left picture). Cut down selected lines **X–Y–R** to the bust points. Close all darts to produce pleats at **X**, **Y** and **R**. Shape side seams to give a tighter fit. Cut under-bodice as for bodice **A**.

Bodice (right picture). Cut down from point **X** to the bust point. Close the side dart and remove the waist dart. Tighten the top edge by cutting a 2cm dart from point **Y**, as illustrated.

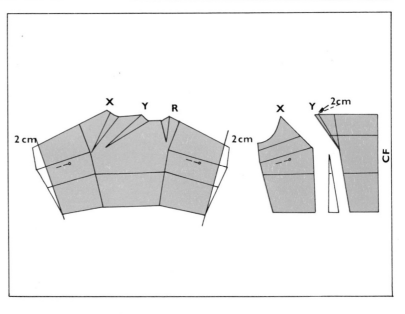

DESIGN DATED 1938

DESIGN JEAN PATOU 1938

a) Draw lines **X–B–C, A–D–C**.
Note: For loose fit draw **A–B–C** only.

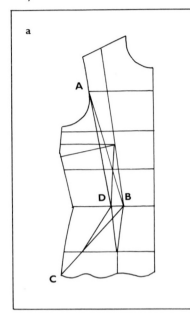

b) Cut the centre and side panels as indicated. Close side bust dart. Add **CF** wrap-over.
Use basic back pattern.

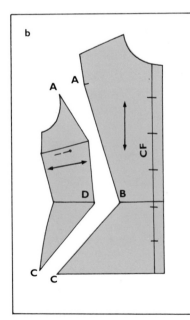

DESIGN 1966

a) Cut from point **X** to the bust point, and close side bust dart.

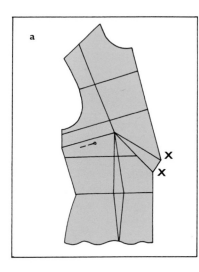

b) Draw side panel, using angled waist darts to retain closer body fitting.
Use basic back pattern.

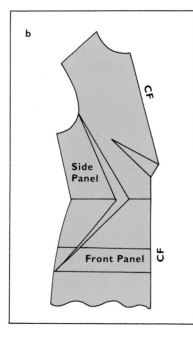

RAISED WAISTLINES 1801–1807

RAISED WAISTLINE

a) Matching the shoulder seams, cut the front and back neckline.

b) Cut through the front and back pattern on lines **X–Y** as illustrated.

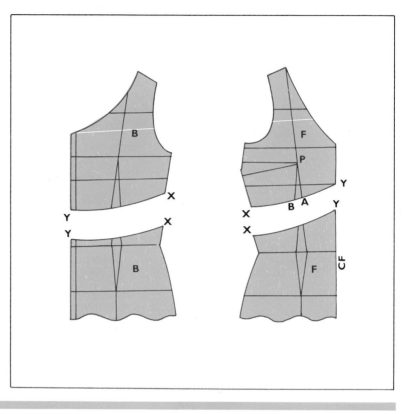

ALTERNATIVE DARTING

Cut out the dart **B–P–A**, and close the side-bust dart. Stitch the increased dart **B–P–A** or gather **X–Y** to fit skirt.
For skirt: see peg-top skirts.

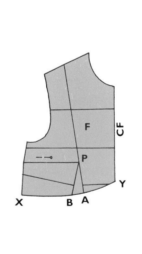

DROPPED WAISTLINE

DROPPED WAISTLINES 1925 AND 1977

Changing the position of the waistline has produced new styling in many periods of history. In the dropped waistline design, the longer bodice often hung loosely to the hip. It is a look created by not using the waist darts. The side-bust dart must be kept, and can be moved to any position. Belts could be used to bring in the natural waist to fit. Trimming, and indeed belts, could be placed on the dropped line to emphasise the cut.

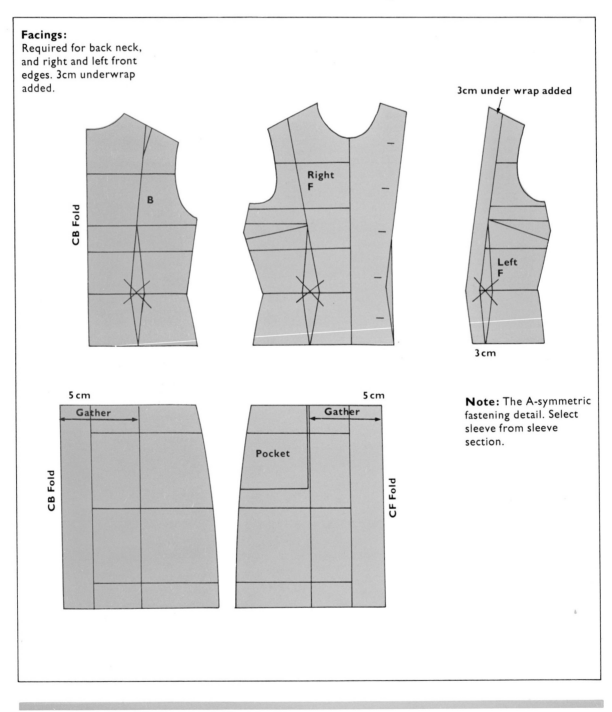

Facings:
Required for back neck, and right and left front edges. 3cm underwrap added.

3cm under wrap added

B

CB Fold

Right F

Left F

3cm

5 cm

Gather

CB Fold

5 cm

Gather

Pocket

CF Fold

Note: The A-symmetric fastening detail. Select sleeve from sleeve section.

DROPPED WAISTLINE

BLOUSON TOP

Back: Cut from **X–Y** and close shoulder dart.

Front: Cut from **A–B**. Close side-bust dart. Straighten side seams.

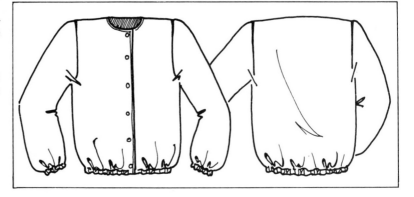

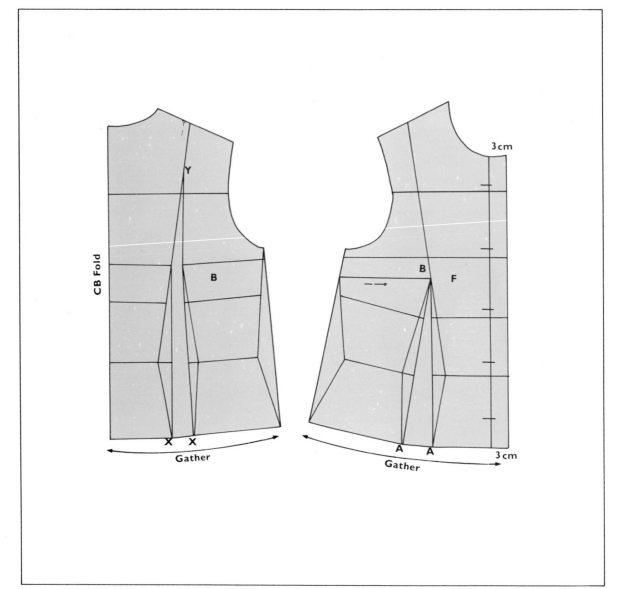

DEEP ARMHOLE

DEEP ARMHOLE

a) Place patterns together, as illustrated. Cut out the waist darts and the shoulder dart.

Close side-bust dart. Draw sleeve.

b) Spread the sleeve to the required fullness. Join bodice pieces together. Back **R–X**. Front **S–A**, to complete the bodice pattern pieces.

Use 4-gore skirt pattern with waist gathers.

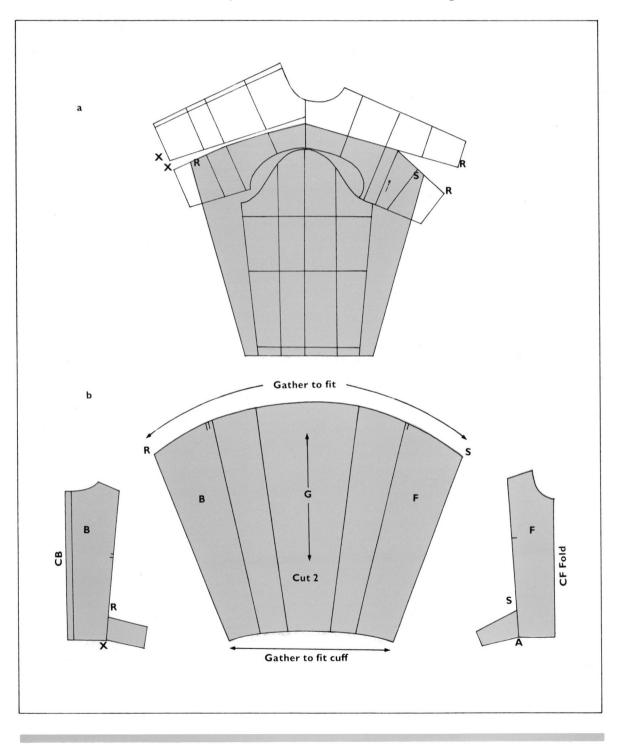

STRAPLESS GOWNS

STRAPLESS GOWNS

For the bodice to stay in position without straps, the pattern has to be well shaped and tight fitting. An underbodice is invariably used, acting as a 'bra' to improve the shape and give further support. Boning could, if so desired, be inserted into the seams to maintain the shape.

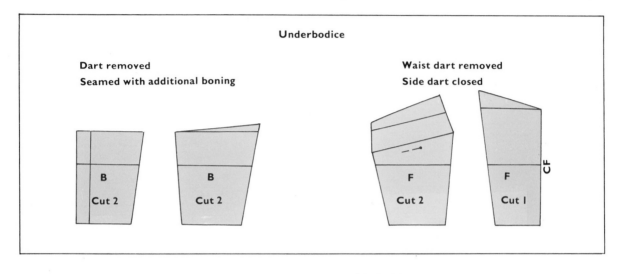

Underbodice

Dart removed
Seamed with additional boning

Waist dart removed
Side dart closed

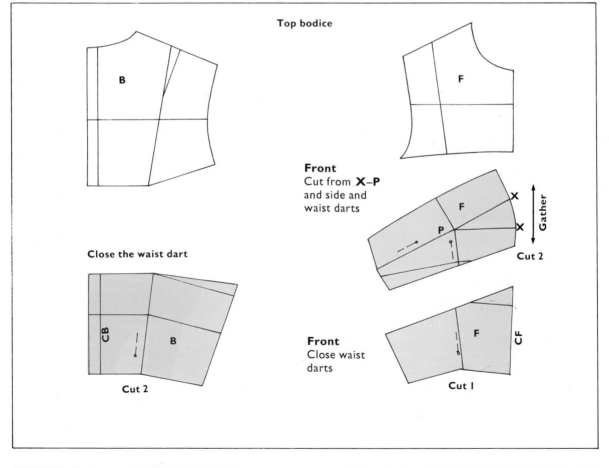

Top bodice

Close the waist dart

Front
Cut from **X–P** and side and waist darts

Front
Close waist darts

LINGERIE DESIGNS

LINGERIE DESIGNS

a) Cut pattern as indicated.

b) Close front side-bust dart by opening the waist dart.

c) Cut out the darts and place skirt together at points **X**. Spread to achieve required hem fullness.

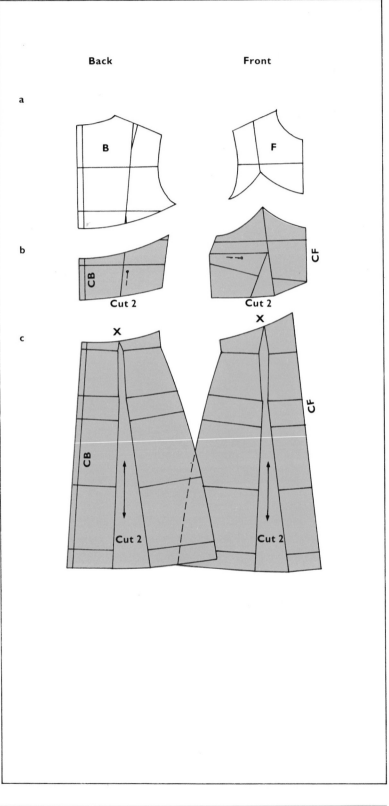

BASIC BRA BLOCK

a) Close front side-bust dart into the shoulder position. Draw bra shape as illustrated.

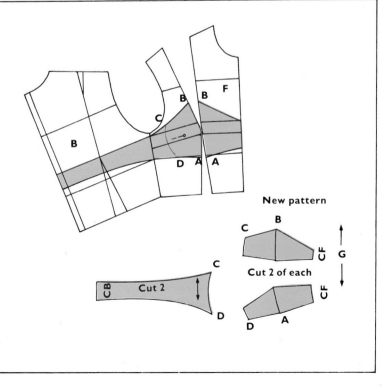

New pattern

Cut 2 of each

Cut 2

HALTER NECK

HALTER NECK

Draw front and back pattern sections as illustrated.

Note: Side seams are reduced by 1.5cm at the top tapering to normal waist.

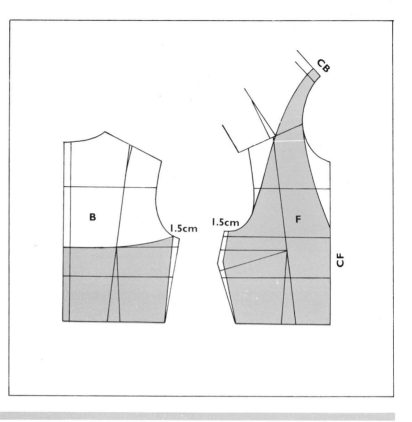

NEW PATTERN

a) Close front side-bust dart, allowing waist dart to open.

b) Close back waist dart.

c) Place patterns together at the side seams and cut as one piece. Fold out optional 2cm dart to tighten the armhole.

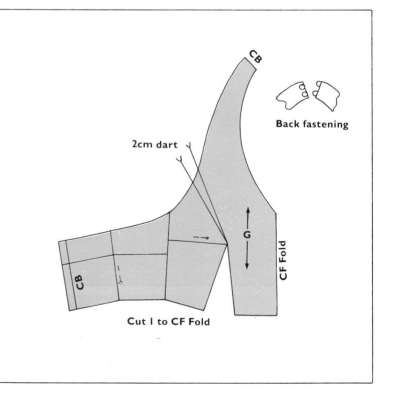

SUN DRESS OR NIGHTGOWN

SUN DRESS (OR NIGHTGOWN)

a) Draw the top band on to your basic pattern. Remove the front side-bust dart. Cut the band from the pattern, and fold out 1.5cm on both the front and back top edge to give a closer fit.

b) Skirt
Spread the front and back skirt, as illustrated to produce the gathers. Straighten side seams.

Hem Frill
Measure the width around the bottom skirt. Select the depth of frill required. Cut frill to exact measurements if no gathers are required. For maximum gathering multiply the width by two.

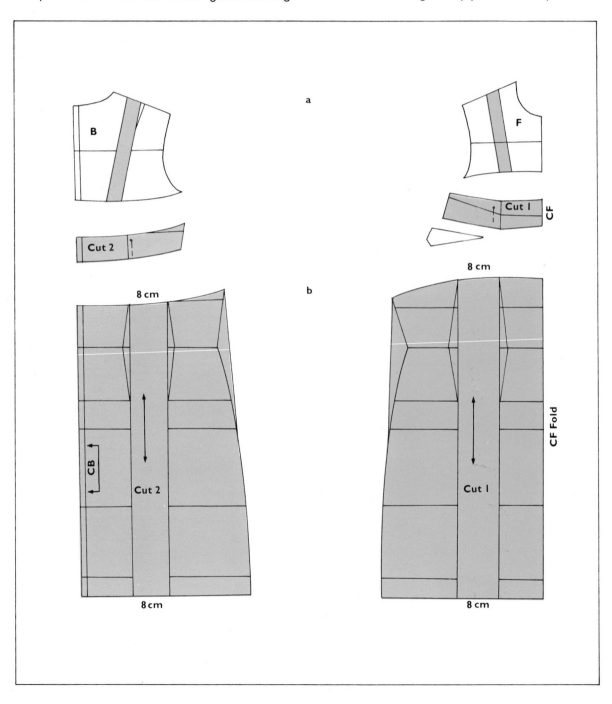

EVENING DRESS

EVENING DRESS

Draw the bodice on to your basic pattern.

Back

Close the dart and also tighten the top edge by 1.5cm.

Front

Draw new dart line. Close side-bust dart and waist dart. Tighten top edge by 1.5cm.

The Skirt

The front and back skirt are slashed and opened, as illustrated.

The side seams **C–R** are straightened. For more pleats or gathers, spread as required.

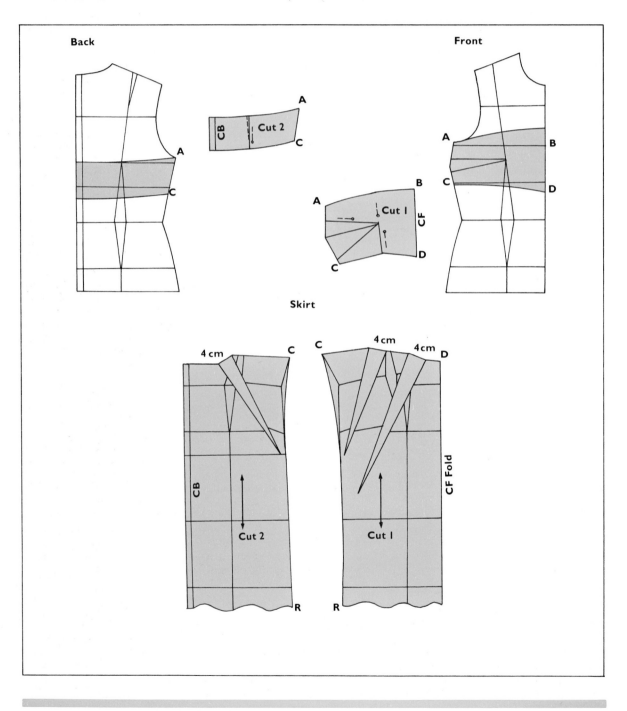

SMOCK BLOUSE

SMOCK BLOUSE

Vest Draw the collar.
A–B = $\frac{1}{2}$ back neck.

Back
Omit waist darts. Flare side seams by 6cm at hem line.

Front
Cut down line **A–P** and close side-bust dart. Remove vest piece **A–P–X**. Extend centre front to **Y**. **X–Y** = 4cm to allow for pleats. Flare side seams by 6cm at hem line. Omit waist darts.

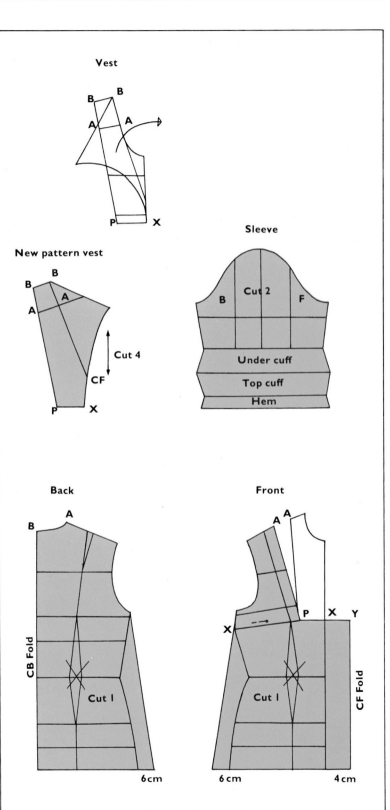

Vest

New pattern vest

Sleeve

Back

Front

GENERAL ABBREVIATIONS

CF	Centre front
CB	Centre back
RS	Right side of fabric
WS	Wrong side of fabric
CF Fold	Place **CF** to fold of fabric
CB Fold	Place **CB** to fold of fabric
↑G↓	Grain of fabric, i.e. the direction in which the pattern pieces should be placed on fabric.

⁓ Shortened version of pattern, to which required length should be added.

←— Pin, representing dart folded out, or dart closed.

F	Front
B	Back
S	Sleeve

All measurements are indicated in centimetres.

EASE

Patterns are not made to body measurements. The basic master pattern has 5cm ease added to all circumference body measurements. **This is called fitting ease**.

Fitting ease varies from the 5cm allowed on the master pattern, to 10–12cm ease on a jacket, and 15–18cm ease on a top coat. The amount of ease required depends upon what you intend tu wear underneath. You would therefore need to increase the size of your blocks for jackets and coats.

Jackets (ease 10cm)
Lower armhole 1.25cm.
Add 1.25cm to side seams.
Adjust sleeves to fit new armhole.

Coats (17cm ease)
Let 1cm strip into **F** and **B** pattern as illustrated.
Lower armholes 2cm.

Add 2cm to side seams.
Adjust sleeves to fit new armhole.

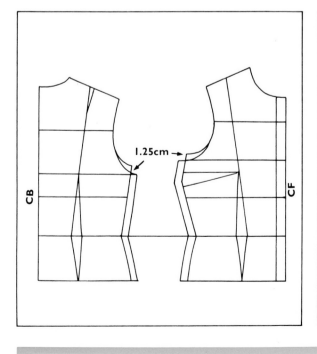

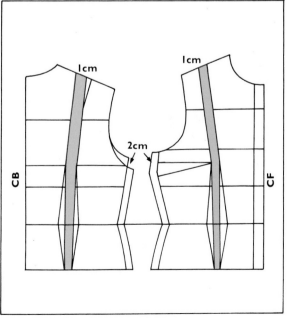

FASHION EASE

Fashion ease is additional to fitting ease, and is totally at the discretion of the designer who decides just how much bigger or tighter a garment should be to achieve a new 'look'.

One of the advantages of a correct master pattern is that you can place any new pattern that you buy on top of the master and see immediately, not only if it is the correct figure-fitting for you, but also how much fashion ease has been added.

If you are making your own patterns it is a good idea to always carry a tape measure so that you can evaluate the width of styles that you see in the ready-to-wear shops.

ADAPTING FROM THE MASTER PATTERN

The master pattern that you have made will have seam allowances wherever necessary. If you cut up the pattern — like a jig-saw puzzle — to produce new styles, the lines that you cut **will not have a seam allowance**, and you should therefore learn immediately that a consistant method of indicating the need to 'add a seam' must be used.

Seams – using a Red Marker
a) Place large **X** marks in *red* on the lines to be cut.

b) When the pattern is cut through the red **V**'s will remind you to **add a seam allowance**, and they will also give you excellent matching points.

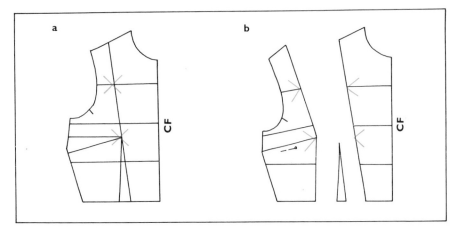

Alternative Method
You should cut away the seam allowances on the master pattern before you start adapting, then remember **to add a seam allowance to all edges**.

In this book I have deliberately left the choice to you. You should notice however that I have always retained the centre back seam and the hem in all diagrams, as I have found that this is a tremendous aid to student's recognition of pattern pieces.

Practice
The quickest way to competent and successful pattern adaption, and dress designing, is to practice with **small scale patterns**. Pads of miniature patterns are available from news-agents and stationers, and a model doll, which comes with it's own master pattern, is also available.

Details from: Betty Foster,
P.O. Box 28
Crewe CW2 6PH

INDEX